View from the Top

By Jim Hough

Published by the
Michigan Electric Cooperative Association
2859 W. Jolly Road, Okemos, MI 48864

VIEW FROM THE TOP

Copyright © 2005 by the Michigan Electric Cooperative Association

Reproduction in whole or in part is strictly prohibited without prior written approval of the Michigan Electric Cooperative Association (MECA), except that reasonable portions may be reproduced or quoted as part of a review or other story about this publication.

Columns previously appeared in *Michigan Country Lines* magazine.

www.countrylines.com

Published by the Michigan Electric Cooperative Association
2859 W. Jolly Road, Okemos, MI 48864

Cover art by Dennis Preston

Book design by Cindy Zuker

Printed in the United States of America by BRD Printing Inc., Lansing, Michigan

Author's note: It's a special treat that this book is printed by my brother Don's company. Wouldn't our dad be proud?

ISBN 0-9776253-0-3

To my wife, Darl

If it has not been nearly 50 years of marital bliss, then I sure came mighty close. As most readers know, I have been legally blind for more than 40 years—unable to drive or read printed material. Although she maintained a 27-year career as a teacher, she also raised two wonderful children, Linda and Steve, and served as my loving wife, cab driver and daily reader. How she managed all that remains a mystery. Thus, this book and any other professional notoriety I enjoy is largely of her creation. I may be a man of words, but they cannot describe my gratitude for the love of such a woman.

Contents

On the Road 11

Special People 42

Along Co-op Lines 79

Bless the Animals 94

Life in the U.P. 119

Family and Friends 164

My View 192

A Word from the Author

I am humbled by the many honors that came my way during a long writing career. Induction into the Michigan Journalism Hall of Fame and the Central Michigan University Journalism Hall of Fame did not put me on an ego trip. Instead they filled me with a special kind of gratitude. Much has been made of my years as a daily columnist for the *Lansing State Journal*. But there is a special place in my journalistic life that belongs to the Michigan Electric Cooperative Association and its magazine, *Country Lines*. Oh, how I loved doing all the columns in this book for the *Country Lines* readers. There is something special about America's rural people and, just like the column's name says, I am 'right at home' when writing for them.

The first *"Right At Home"* book, published about 10 years ago, is long out of print because you bought 5,000 of them. Profits went to scholarships for rural kids, and so it will be with this book. A special thanks to Mike Buda and the Michigan Electric Cooperative Association staff for support and encouragement. In my retirement years, you've enriched my life and, more importantly, kept me from going brain-dead.

Jim Hough

From the Editor

Research shows that half of the people who read magazines start at the back. I'm one of them. It isn't logical; it just seems easier to skim the pages that way. It's also the fastest way to get to interesting nuggets the publishers stick there to lure readers to the back pages, where often not much happens except advertising. For *Country Lines* magazine, that lure is Jim Hough's column, "Right at Home." And judging by the volume of mail Jim gets, the lure works very well.

Jim Hough has been touching *Country Lines* readers with his humor, empathy, and insight for more than 20 years. Before he became the unofficial cheerleader for Michigan's electric cooperatives, rural residents and the Upper Peninsula, he was a force in Lansing through his column for the *Lansing State Journal*. We were fortunate to keep him writing for us after he retired early from the newspaper because of vision problems. It's apparent that the members of electric cooperatives, who get the magazine and who continue to enjoy Jim's writing, agree that he is a welcome visitor in our homes each month.

This collection of columns from the past 10 years follows an earlier collection called *Right at Home* that quickly sold out in 1995. This book demonstrates once again the rapport and respect Jim shares with readers, whether he is writing of his love for friends and family, his trips with his dear wife and driver, Darl, his observations of life in the Upper Peninsula or his reflections on what life ought to be.

We are proud to call him "friend," and suspect that, because of him, more people now start reading from the back of the magazine.

Mike Buda, Editor

On The Road

View From The Top

September/October 1999

I couldn't believe it. There I was, standing at the top of a Mackinac Bridge tower—552 feet above the water.

It was so exciting that I was all the way back down on firm ground before I remembered that I have a fear of heights.

Even more amazing is that this northwestern tower of the Big Mac was officially named "The Jim Hough Tower" 30 years ago.

It all began in my days as a daily columnist for the *Lansing State Journal*. Our family made many trips to our Lake Superior cottage at Paradise and the bridge toll—then $3.75—was a big hurt. I wrote lots of columns urging state legislators to lower the toll. Soon, many got people on board and a movement was about to remove that economic barrier.

When I wrote that I had paid enough in bridge tolls to pay for one of those bridge towers, the Mackinac Bridge Authority sent me a certificate officially naming the northwest tower "The Jim Hough Tower."

Their effort was good for my ego, but it didn't stop the flow of words from my typewriter and, in 1969, the state refinanced the bridge and lowered the toll to $1.50 where it has been for the past 30 years.

Recently, I learned that there is an elevator in that northwest tower so I contacted Hank Lotoszinski, executive secretary of the Mackinac Bridge Authority. I told him I wanted to climb my tower.

"You are in luck, Jim," Hank said. "Under normal circumstances, I'd say no to that. But I had a long career in Lansing with the Michigan Department of Transportation and I read your column for years. What say I take you up there personally?"

So, on June 21, 1999, I found myself climbing out of a hatch cover on a platform 552 feet above the water. For minutes I was speechless. It was awesome. Looking down at the traffic flowing below, huge trucks looked like ants. I was afraid to move. Hank told me his crew provides a driver service each year for more than 4,000 people who are too afraid to drive over the bridge and here I stood, a partially-sighted 67-year-old reporter with arthritis, standing way up there. Wow!

In a few minutes, another head popped out of that hatch. I turned to help him out. It was a special and a proud moment for me because that person was the great Lawrence Rubin, a.k.a Mr. Mackinac Bridge, a legend in these parts.

Larry, now 86, wanted to make the trip up there with me. That climb is a serious physical challenge and Larry's knees don't respond as well anymore. It took minutes before he got his breath and got to his feet. I feared I had caused him big trouble.

"No, Jim, I have not been up here in many years and this will surely be my last time. But I wanted to do it with you. Have you ever seen anything so beautiful?"

It was a beautiful, quiet and sunny day and it was a time I will always treasure. What a treat it was to visit up there with those two men—the old and the new commanders of the longest bridge in the northern hemisphere.

All went well until Hank pointed down at the bridge

roadway and said, "In high winds, Jim, the bridge sways as much as 35 feet in one direction. It takes two to three hours to swing and the same to come back." That did it. "Let's get back down," I said.

Going up was hardest. You are 200 feet above the water on the roadway when you enter a narrow hatchway through which you pass with one leg and one arm at a time. You get into the world's smallest elevator and ride up more than 200 feet. You emerge from that elevator and begin a narrow ladder climb of about 50 feet to the top. You pass through several rounded openings that refuse admission to anyone who's overweight.

It is scary, claustrophobic and demands a bundle of physical agility. For Larry and me, it was almost too much. But we did it. At the bottom, I put a hug on him.

What a man Larry Rubin is. He was appointed executive secretary of the bridge authority in 1950, eight years before the bridge was completed. He retired after nearly 34 years in that post. He has produced videos, films and books on the Mighty Mac. One book, "Bridging the Straits," has sold more than 40,000 copies. Upon retirement, Larry built a home on a St. Ignace bluff overlooking his bridge. He still serves as a hospital board trustee, and as a member of the Historical Center Foundation. Currently, he is leading a drive to build a new library in St. Ignace. They should have named that bridge "The Rubin." They didn't. I sure hope that new library bears his name. I'd be at that dedication ceremony.

Oh, by the way, Hank Lotoszinski says it's occasionally possible for members of the public to go up the tower, but only for high bidders in charity auctions or under rare and special circumstances. Charities interested can write to Hank. They won't have any more trouble with me. I'd be chicken to do it again.

No Exception To The Rule

May/June 1995

Every now and then, a great day can suddenly turn into a nightmare. I was reminded of that last summer on a country road 40 miles north of Newberry.

Paradise friends, Jim and Jerry Patt, had joined us in a little vacation trip with travel trailers. We had set up camp at a beautiful remote state forest campground at Culhane Lake. Then we went blueberry picking.

Jim was driving my vehicle as we worked our way to historic, abandoned Chris Point Lighthouse on Lake Superior. It was a few miles up Luce County Road 412—a sandy, two-track road.

Suddenly, a young lad on a trail bike (small motorcycle) roared around a curve at high speed. He spotted our car, which was well to the right side of the road, but he was heading at top speed for our front end. With hearts in our throats, we watched as he managed to dive off the trail bike and skid on the roadway past our car. His trail bike crashed into the front of our vehicle.

We all rushed to the boy, and found him a bit hysterical but without serious injury. Following along behind him were his parents and a sister, each riding a trail bike.

The father confessed that he had no insurance on his trail bikes and that his boy was underage to be driving such a rig on a county road.

I figured I'd better call my AAA insurance company. The nearest phone was at the federal Little Lake Harbor refuge a mile away. It was late Saturday afternoon. AAA insisted that it was critical for us to get a police report of the accident. Meanwhile, the Indiana family returned to their campsite somewhere on the Two Hearted River.

I called the Luce County sheriff's office. A sleepy voice said: "I'm sorry mister, I'm just the jailer. We have nobody here to take an accident report. You'll have to call the State Police post in Newberry."

I called the State Police post where a trooper said: "Well, we close the post at 5 p.m. We'll make a report if you can get here before 5 p.m."

I couldn't believe it. "Hey, wait a minute," I said. "Whatever happened to law enforcement and public service? Are you asking me to make an 80-mile round trip? How will you investigate this accident in the comfort of your offices?"

The trooper muttered something about state budget restraints, shortage of patrol cars and troopers and concluded with a clear assertion: Come to us or you get no police report of the accident.

So off we roared to Newberry, arriving at the police post a few minutes after 5 p.m. A trooper was just locking the door. I slammed my fist on the glass for him to open up. He did.

When we had finished telling our version of the event, I asked if they would then go investigate further and visit the other parties to the crash.

"Not likely, because there seem to be no serious injuries," the trooper said.

I called AAA again and they said I should get a bumper shop estimate of repair costs and let them know. Over the next few days, at a major inconvenience to us, we got estimates that our car repairs would be nearly $1,000 and our only car would be out of service for a couple of days.

A couple of weeks later, Denny's Collision Shop at Newberry called to say they had the parts and were ready to repair our vehicle. I called AAA. They sent us a check made out to Denny's Collision and to us jointly. Trouble was, the check was $250 short of the repair estimate. "That $250 is your deductible," AAA said. AAA seemed to be saying we were at fault since they had no official police information to the contrary. Remember now that the State Police did not investigate the accident or talk to the other parties. They only filled out an accident report form with information we hauled to them in an 80-mile round trip to their offices.

After several angry phone calls, AAA finally paid the deductible—as well they should have from day one.

Six months later, Darl and I were traveling with the same vehicle when we hit what is called "black ice" in the Upper Peninsula. The thin layer of ice on blacktop pavement is created by lake-effect showers in winter. Although we were traveling under 30 miles an hour, our car suddenly spun out of control and slid into a guardrail. There was no injury or involvement with other cars, but there was $1,400 in damage—same left fender, bumper and grill we had just repaired.

The nightmare from that experience came after we had the car repaired. AAA said they were putting a $145 annual surcharge on our policy because of the accident. What's more, the surcharge would stay on our policy for at least three years.

That spurred real anger. Here's why:

1. Darl and I have had AAA insurance since 1957—38 years.

2. That black ice fender bender was the first "chargeable" accident we had ever had. "Chargeable" is a term used by insurance companies even when there is no ticket issued. It means the driver did not have the car under control.

I was furious. I called AAA and went through several underlings until I finally got to the chief claims agent. I asked whatever happened to insurance companies that rewarded drivers for 38 years of safe driving. He said the 38 years didn't count anymore. He said that current state law makes them place surcharges on drivers in such circumstances. When I threatened to quit AAA he warned me that their policies were no different than other companies, although some companies "granted a little more leniency in the matter."

Not giving up, I called the State of Michigan insurance commissioner. Sure enough, that's the deal. I wonder how many folks like me don't know that. The bottom line is that you can drive safely for half a century until you make a slight goof in which you have to pay your deductible for car repairs and suddenly your insurance company will fine you by raising your insurance premium 25 percent.

Where were all of us when they passed that law? The AAA claims supervisor told me he agreed that we had a strong complaint and a great case in point but that he was unable to make an exception under the current AAA rules.

As you can see, I'm still angry.

Trash Stalkin'

July/August 1995

A sensational and generous thing has been going on in Michigan for the past five years that many of us take for granted.

I refer to beautiful roadsides in our state resulting from our "Adopt-A-Highway" project. Nearly 50,000 volunteers put in more than 15,000 hours picking up trash along nearly 7,000 miles of our state's highways last year. They removed 112,000 bags of trash.

All that warms me these days as I travel in retirement and notice some disgusting roadsides in other states. I thought it time to yell out a loud thanks to all our pride-filled Michigan folks. So I went to visit an old friend, Bill Rintamaki, district permits agent for the Michigan Department of Transportation at Newberry.

"Whenever I think our country is going to heck in a handbasket, I see all those wonderful people out there working very, very hard in a kind of dirty job just so the rest of us can feast our eyes on a beautiful roadside," said Bill, a 29-year state employee.

To make his point, Bill introduced me to Joyce Jones Kujat of rural St. Ignace. She, her husband, Mike, and their 12 children adopted five miles of highway on US-2, west of St. Ignace. She put it this way:

"My husband, Lockwood (Bud) Jones, was a state highway employee for 22 years until he died in 1976, leaving me with seven children. Later, I met Mike Kujat, a school bus driver who was left with five children when his wife, Joanne, died. After we were married, we each looked for some way to do a memorial to Bud and Joanne.

"We decided to adopt a highway in their honor. State highway signs at each end of the five-mile stretch read: In memorial to Lockwood Bud Jones and Joanne Kujat.

"Mike and I and our 12 kids picked up 48 bags of trash that first time and then we had a potluck dinner to reminisce about Bud and Joanne. It was a beautiful thing then and it is still going on three times a year. It brings us a lot of family warmth and it enhances US-2, one of the most beautiful highways in the state as it runs along the Lake Michigan shoreline. We hope to continue it forever," she said.

In their last venture in April, the family picked up 12 bags of trash.

"I get a little angry at people who toss stuff out their car windows," Joyce said. "They stop in St. Ignace for fast food and then throw the containers and paper out as they head west on US-2."

Most common trash includes pop and beer cans and bottles, disposable diapers, fast food trash wrappers, tires, mufflers, and a variety of paper wrappings.

"Perhaps the most unusual thing we ever found was 100 boxes of Ex-Lax. We figured they either fell off a delivery truck or else somebody had a very, very big problem," she said.

Rintamaki supervises Adopt-A-Highway groups for his district, the eastern six counties of the Upper Peninsula.

"I have 116 groups taking care of 396 miles of highways and they make me very proud. Studies show that Michigan's roadside litter dropped by 40 percent after we passed the bottle return law in 1978 and they show a 30-percent reduction on top of that since Adopt-A-Highway began five years ago," he said.

Although 48 states have some form of Adopt-A-Highway, few do it as successfully as Michigan.

"When the program began statewide five years ago, there were 824 groups with six or more persons signed up. Today, we have 3,048 groups. What's more, the program has staying power, as 544 of those original groups are still with us," Bill said.

Although most Adopt-A-Highway signs recognize service clubs, businesses and organizations, any group of six or more people can adopt a highway. Pick up projects are scheduled three times a year in April, July and September.

Groups are allowed to keep and collect deposit money on all bottles and cans. On her last venture, Joyce said she returned 100 cans worth $10.

"Fortunately, we don't have to transport all that trash," Joyce said, "because the state sends a truck along later to pick up the bags. They also furnish us with orange vests and safety training."

Last year, a Wayne County group found two crisp $100 bills. A Harley motorcycle club in Bay County found an uncashed check for $5,352.43, dated 1977, and a car title for a 1983 Pontiac from Menominee County. An Imlay City group found a bank deposit bag containing checks and credit receipts from a gas station robbery.

* * * * *

There is another side to Bill Rintamaki—a great sense of humor. He established and copyrighted "Hug a Snow Flea, Snow Flea Protection Society," complete with logo and literature.

Folks downstate think the snow flea is a myth. But any reliable reference book on entomology will describe it. It's just that Rintamaki carries it a bit further.

"We live with the snow fleas all winter," he says, "but they are especially prominent on the snow on warm, sunny spring days."

All that is true enough, but Rintamaki, a native Yooper, likes to put folks on. As part of a celebration of Newberry's centennial, Bill invented and then "planted" a news story that even fooled the Associated Press, which sent it around the world:

NEWBERRY—A birch-bark scroll recently discovered in the northern part of Luce County has piqued the interest of a group of local businessmen who are undertaking to solve an apparent mystery as to its origin.

Ron Hermanson, one of the group, said the find is among the most intriguing archeological finds in Luce County.

Hermanson said it is particularly appropriate that the discovery was made in Newberry's centennial year, adding that the group suspects the message found on the bark to be ancient hieroglyphics of obscure Algonquian Indian origin. The group is seeking a cryptologist who would be able to decipher the code.

Local analysis of the scroll's content indicates one part of the message refers to the Algonquian term "eekuel" meaning, according to some, "little biter" in an apparent reference to the snow flea. The insect infested the area by the millions—making life miserable for human inhabitants.

Getting Away

March/April 1998

A city dweller friend of mine recently ventured into my northland lair for a visit. When he reached my area, he tried to call me on his cellular car phone. No luck.

In my driveway, he got out of his car, slammed the door in disgust and said: This may be Paradise to you, Jim, but all I have seen is trees. Hell, man, my cellular phone won't even work up here."

"Yeah, I know. Isn't it great?" I said.

It is great, indeed. I'm darned proud to live in the only area of Michigan where a cellular phone won't work. They keep promising the cell phone folks to put up some towers to cover the area northwest of Paradise but, fortunately, they haven't done it yet.

Go west of Paradise along Lake Superior and you find 100-plus miles of wilderness—still unprofitable for cell phone merchants. Isn't it great? At least a tiny part of the state hasn't been thus far spoiled by such modern contraptions.

I'm getting at bit worried, though, because they recently installed a new tower at Eckerman and the Paradise area. They work—on occasion. But I can still go a few miles north of Newberry where I'm delighted to find my cell phone won't work.

Oh yeah, I forgot to mention that I have a car phone, too. But I often use mine for a different purpose—to find areas in the United States where they won't work. Last year, my wife, Darl, and I found several wonderful places in the wilds of Texas and the Ozark Mountains of Arkansas where the car phone wouldn't work. Each time we could be sure we were in a splendid, remote wilderness where city dwellers were uncomfortable.

Readers who are used to my byline know I'm exaggerating this a little. But there is much truth in it, too.

After cell phones will come condos on our wilderness shores. How sad all that would be—for everyone in our state.

We bought a car phone several years ago because we travel the nation's highways a lot. Because of my blindness, Darl has to do all the driving and we felt the car phone offered some highway security in an emergency. It also gives our family a chance to find us in our travels--providing we have not hidden away in the Ozark Mountains.

Once, I recall, we used our car phone to get immediate help for a family seriously injured in a car crash. Thus, I am a car phone fan, but I admit I like them best where they don't work.

Speaking of Texas and Arkansas, I should take this moment to explain why we have gone to those areas in recent winters.

Years ago, I thought the Upper Peninsula winters were spectacular. Now, with my vision problems and a touch of arthritis, I find it less fun to run my snowblower twice a day and then retreat into my Lake Superior cabin to a talking book or satellite TV. Heck, it's dark by five o'clock each evening. Cabin fever sets in.

So, we have hooked onto our travel trailer and headed south. What a blast it is to leave those 20-foot snowdrifts for a lawn chair in the beautiful sun on the Gulf of Mexico at South Padre Island. We put on our chest-high waders, walk out into the crashing ocean surf and cast a line from a 12-foot fishing rod. Then we return to the beach, place the rod in a holder, sit down in a lawn chair, open a refreshment and wait for the rod tip to start jumping.

We have caught as many as 30 ocean fish in a day—whiting, pompano, sheephead, drum, and more. Compare that to bleak skies and snow shoveling.

Trouble is, we have a lot of company. The population in the Rio Grand Valley of Texas swells in the winter months in an unbelievable way. You need a travel trailer park or condo reservation many months in advance. We stay in a nice trailer park at Port Isabel, Texas, for $140 per month. Heck, it would cost me more in firewood to stay up north and fight depression.

After a couple of months in Texas, we work our way north—not in a hurry. We visit spectacular cities like Corpus Christy, Galveston and San Antonio. We stop for a few weeks in a remote campground in Arkansas to fish for crappies and bass. We like to be back in Paradise in time for smelt fishing.

* * * * *

Last spring, we had to come home a couple of weeks early and, on April 20, had to get my friend, Irv Bolz, to clean out my driveway with his tractor and plow. On the third week of April, we still had nearly two feet of snow in our yard. Ridiculous. The major league baseball season had been underway for two weeks elsewhere.

A postscript to explain why we came home early last spring. You may recall a column I wrote in *Country Lines* several years ago about my old journalism professor at Central Michigan University. I went back to the University to speak to the journalism students and found that Gilbert Maienknecht had been forgotten there, even though he founded and nurtured the journalism school. A list of the now famed journalists he spawned there is dazzling. In that column, I said Dr. Maienknecht belonged in the Michigan Journalism Hall of Fame. With lots of help, I began a campaign to put him there. While in Texas, I learned that he would be honored in East Lansing on April 19 in an induction ceremony placing him in the Hall of Fame.

"We're goin' home early," I told my wife, "and if you won't take me, I'm gonna walk to East Lansing."

What a proud moment that was for all of us. Gilbert Maienknecht in the Michigan Journalism Hall of Fame—right where he belongs.

Small World

January/February 1999

Yes, it is a small world and I have always been fascinated by small world stories. Everybody has one to tell.

My wife, Darl, and I left Paradise with our travel trailer in early January to spend some time in Texas last winter. Our close friends, Jim and Jerry Patt, left Paradise in late February with their trailer to spend time in New Mexico. On our way home in April, we stopped at a highway rest area on Highway I-10 near the Louisiana-Texas border. There they were, Jim and Jerry, stopped at the same rest area, en route to visit a relative in Louisiana!

Good grief, what are the odds against that?

Almost as weird was an incident two years ago with other close friends, Jerry and Evelyn Brehm of Brimley. The Brehms came to visit us for a goodbye dinner, since we were leaving for Texas for a winter trip. Jerry and Evelyn were leaving for Gulf Shores, Alabama, but weren't sure of their departure date. Darl and I pulled into a travel trailer park at Elizabethtown, Kentucky, the next week and registered at the office for a lot assignment. We pulled up to that lot and parked—right next to Jerry and Evelyn! Figure those odds.

* * * * *

Another Paradise friend, Jerry Marsden, recently asked me: "What compels folks like you to leave the winter splendor of Michigan's Upper Peninsula?"

It's hard for a travel trailer bug to explain all that to the uninitiated.

Yooper winters are surely beautiful and I have lived through many of them. But in recent years, they are a bit too long for me. It gets dark about 5 p.m. And the days get short and the nights long. For a nearly-blind guy like me, a talking book diet can only go so far before cabin fever makes a violent attack in February. So we head out to do some surf fishing on South Padre Island in Texas. En route, we see a lot of the United States and visit some old friends.

Fortunately for me, I married a clever woman 44 years ago. She was a long-time school teacher, but I think she should have been an 18-wheeler driver. She hauls our travel trailer about 5,000 miles each year with great expertise. Male macho types marvel as she backs our trailer perfectly into trailer lots or whips it through downtown Atlanta, Indianapolis, Houston and Washington, D.C. She's something. But that shouldn't surprise anyone because an amazing number of big trucks running over our nation's highways today are driven by women. Most big trucking companies are busy recruiting women drivers. That's because they are darned good at it.

But back to the point of all this...we find a ton of fun in the nation's travel trailer parks. You meet some of the greatest people, all reduced to one thing in common. On one side of you may be a bank president or doctor. On the other side may be the school janitor or a broken-down old newspaper columnist. Travel trailer parks in the Rio Grande Valley and other southern places become a winter melting pot of America's nicest people, all in relaxed mode and eager to know each other.

Those Crazy Americans

November/December 1999

Loco is the Spanish word for crazy, and that's what they called us in one Mexican city—"loco Americanos."

I guess it's fair to say we earned that reputation as crazy Americans when my wife, Darl, and I and our friends Bill and Carol Perry hauled a metal suit of armor that measured seven feet tall from deep in the heart of Matamoros, Mexico, to the Texas border—lashed to a small shopping cart.

Why in the world did we do all that? Well, it all began back in Michigan's Upper Peninsula last December when Darl and I had our annual physical exams by our beloved doctor, Kimberly "Kim" Hanert of Newberry.

Doc Hanert learned we were going to Texas for the winter and remarked about her fascination with those tin sculptured armor suits that stand life-size as ornaments.

"I always wanted one of those things for my home, but they are too large to take home on the airplane or to ship home by UPS," she said.

We didn't say anything to Kim at the time, but her comment sent Darl and me on a mission: Find a tin man for Kim.

Weeks later, we were deep in the central part of Matamoros, a giant border city across from Brownsville, Texas. There, standing proudly in front of a store in the city market area was the huge metal sculpture we wanted. I can speak some Spanish, so I found the store owner and began a negotiation. He wanted $190. I got him well down from that figure before I realized I could never carry that monster over the Rio Grande River and out of Mexico to Michigan. I gave up.

Later, back at our trailer park at Port Isabel, Texas, I

remembered that my pal, Bill Perry of Marquette, had a cargo trailer he was planning to take back to Marquette in the spring.

I told Bill of my wish to dazzle my doctor and asked if he'd take the giant tin man to Marquette in his trailer.

"Great idea, Jim, let's take Darl and Carol to Mexico and get that bugger," said Bill.

So the great tin man saga began. We took our little fold-up shopping cart across the border, got into a taxi and went a mile or more deep into the city. We found the metal man, standing proudly in the same spot.

I got the store owner down to $115 on condition that he'd hire a truck to take it to the border for us.

"The heck with that," Bill said, "Jim will give you $100 and we'll take it to the border." As the store owner agreed, I stared at Bill in disbelief. "How do you figure we'll get this thing to the border? He won't fit into a taxi," I said.

"We'll get him on a city bus. They all go back to the border eventually on the routes," Bill said.

So we lashed the tall metal man onto our little cart with rope and packaging tape as a large crowd gathered. Tuned to the Spanish conversation around us, I heard "loco Americanos" several times.

Before beginning an eight-block trip to a bus stop, Bill figured we'd better arm ourselves with a couple of margaritas and he aimed our cargo at a very fancy restaurant, "Las Dos Republicas."

I figured they'd deny us entry but the owner, Raul Melguizo, ushered us in and seated us in the crowded and beautiful restaurant.

"Is your metal man sleeping? Does he have a name?" he asked.

I figured he needed a name. Let's see now, Doctor Kim's dad is Jim, and I am Jim, and Jim in Spanish is "Jamie" (pronounced heimee.) Darl gave Jamie a last name, "Cortez," the guy who conquered Mexico dressed in one of those suits a long time ago.

We left the restaurant to find a city bus, Bill flagged one

down and quickly ushered Darl and Carol aboard. Bill took Jamie's head and I took his feet and, with great difficulty, banged and scrunched him through the narrow door and into the bus center aisle. The bus was full of riders, many of them kids who squealed with delight. I tried to pay the driver. "Please, senor, just go sit down," he said with a roll of his eyes. Once again, I heard several comments about loco Americanos.

We made it to the border but the driver had us stay put until the bus emptied. Then he opened the rear emergency door to let us out with our giant cargo. I shoved a $5 bill into his pocket. I liked him.

Two Mexican cops on bicycles and wearing sidearms stopped us.

"Where are you going with that?" one asked. "We are taking him to Marquette, Michigan," I said. For a minute I feared we were in trouble, but the cop grinned widely and said: "Does he have papers? Is he a wetback?"

I told him the metal man would sink if he tried to swim the Rio Grande. After a good belt of laughter the cops waved us on.

After a long, hard trip across the bridge, through customs and to our truck in the Brownsville parking lot, we finally made it back to Port Isabel and put Jamie to bed for a couple of months.

But the best line of all, I think, came when we pushed and carried the metal man over the Rio Grande bridge in a terrible hot sun. Bill Perry stopped on the bridge, wiped his sweating brow, and said: "Man alive, Jim, she must be a heck of a doctor." She is indeed.

Doctor Kim, of course, had no idea about any of this so it was a real blast when we went to Marquette and removed Jamie, all bound up in cardboard and duct tape, from Bill's trailer. When we arrived at Kim's home in Newberry, we unloaded Jamie and unveiled him before her and her children. The kids all had squeals of delight. Kim had a tear.

For four loco Americanos, Bill, Carol, Darl, and me, it all meant great memories of fun in retirement.

Brake Sense

January/February 2000

Stomp on 'em. You've got to stomp right on 'em."

That was the advice offered to all users of antilock brakes when I rode on a test track near Brimley. In the cab of our truck was Howard Linville, general manager of the Brimley development center for Continental Teves, the folks behind most of the world's antilock brakes technology.

"The biggest problem is not the testing and development of this great modern brake equipment. The biggest problem is retraining the average driver who's been taught to avoid a skid by pumping the brakes. Tell your readers to stomp on their brakes. The equipment will then do the pumping action with far greater efficiency," Linville said.

Early in my visit at the world's largest such test grounds, I realized these folks had made an enormous investment to be sure they are perfect.

The Brimley testing grounds and facilities are valued at more than $7 million and include offices and garages with more than 47,000 square feet. Out on the testing track, there are 19 special road surfaces, including ice, gravel, asphalt, cement, tile and more. Another $1 million will soon be spent there.

"This year, we even added a snow-making machine," Linville said. "Winter testing, especially on ice and snow, is a major effort for us, and last year and the winter before let us down by being historically mild. So we went to a ski resort and brought in a snow-making machine. The Chippewa County winters are usually stormy enough and we may never use that snow-maker, but we have too much at stake to take chances," he said.

Continental Teves, Inc., a leader in antilock brakes technology, contracts with all the world's auto and truck manufacturers. The company, previously known as ITT, is the result of the merger of German companies Continental Tire of Hanover and Teves Brakes Company of Frankfort. The U.S. headquarters of Continental Teves is at Michigan's Auburn Hills.

"This Brimley facility is critical to it all because every new system installed on every new automotive product demands endless testing to perfect performance," Linville said.

"Let's say, for instance, that the Chrysler company is planning a new product, a vehicle that may not be manufactured for several years. They contract with us to perfect a brake system that will work on the vehicle. Our engineers spend endless hours with the Chrysler engineers until that perfection in the brake system is achieved."

That explains the secrecy and security around the Brimley building. A sign in the entrance warns: "No cameras."

"We are contracting and working daily with competing car companies and our integrity is vital to them. Industrial espionage is always a concern to the automotive business and we are awfully careful to keep our integrity intact," Linville said.

I asked Linville to explain the operation of antilock brakes as simply as possible. He gave long thought and responded this way:

"ABS has been around since the 1930s as an idea, but in the late 1970s the micro computer made the theory a reality. Before ABS, drivers were taught to pump the brakes to avoid a skid. The idea was to keep the brakes from locking up and creating additional skid. What the ABS does is pump those brakes for you, but at many, many more times per second than you could with your foot. Each of the four wheels is equipped with sensors that determine the speed of the wheel as it turns. A hydraulic control then opens and closes to reduce or increase the brake pressure on each wheel. Individual wheel control like that is vital because of the grip each wheel may have on the road surface—one may be on gravel and the other on pavement or ice. ABS can't change ice or gravel. Ice is still slippery. But ABS can do wonderful things to optimize the wheel's use of the available grip on that surface."

Thus, the need for such an elaborate testing area like the one at Brimley. "We need about 20 special surfaces so we can test brakes under the exact conditions each time, but we also need miles of regular road surfaces that duplicate the experience of the average driver. Most of our testing does not involve extreme driving moves. Instead, we try to duplicate actions of the average driver. After all, that's what all this is about—the average driver in the world," Linville said.

He repeated his challenge to drivers. "Stand on your brakes. Don't worry about any grinding noise or pulsating actions. They only mean that your ABS system is working perfectly."

Museum Honors Great Lakes Sailors

May/June 2000

For many years, a bright light has flashed every 14 seconds through the bedroom window of my Lake Superior home. It used to irritate me, but now I've grown fond of it.

That's why it was a warm and festive moment last fall when hundreds of folks gathered at Whitefish Point to celebrate the 150th birthday of the oldest lighthouse on Lake Superior. The light, commissioned by Abe Lincoln, was officially turned over to the Great Lakes Shipwreck Historical Society by the Coast Guard.

Who knows how many lives that old blinker has saved? The Lake Superior shoreline from Whitefish Point to Munising has long been known as "The Graveyard of Superior," because hundreds of ships have sunk in storms along that route. Perhaps the most famous was the *Edmund Fitzgerald*, which went down 15 miles from the lighthouse.

Even though the Great Lakes Shipwreck Historical Society now owns the lighthouse, it will continue to function as a vital cog in marine safety. Although the modern inventions of radar, loran, global positioning systems and better weather forecasting have taken over, the Whitefish Point beacon still ranks high with mariners.

Over 87,000 visitors walked under that light last summer—a testimonial to the aura and charm this historical spot represents.

I have watched the growth and popularity of the Shipwreck Museum with amazement. The old Coast Guard lifeboat station died there in about 1950, after 30 years of service. But a junior high school science teacher from Sault Ste. Marie brought new life to Whitefish Point in 1978.

Tom Farnquist grew up with a fascination for things lying below the Lake Superior surface. “As a kid I spent all day in the lake and came out shivering in the evening. As I grew older, I took up scuba diving and began research on Lake Superior shipwrecks,” Farnquist said. Soon, he was doing underwater filming with some friends and the whole subject of shipwreck preservation became more important to him.

In 1978, Farnquist established the Great Lakes Shipwreck Historical Society and, in 1983, that organization made an agreement with the Coast Guard to take over property at Whitefish Point and preserve its history.

Although that grant of federal land was vital, the Historical Society has remained a private nonprofit organization. Today, its annual operating budget is $1.6 million and there are big plans for the future.

“We plan to raise about $5 million for new construction and historical preservation,” Farnquist said. “We want to add two wings to our museum—one for a Great Lakes mariners’ memorial with the names of about 6,000 people who lost their lives on the Great Lakes. A second wing will contain a new auditorium and exhibition area to show off traveling exhibitions and special displays and events,” he explained.

The Great Lakes Shipwreck Historical Society operation eventually became much more than a volunteer effort for Farnquist. He resigned his school teaching post and became the organization’s full-time director.

In recent years, the Society has teamed up with the National Geographic Society and other world famous exploring and historical groups to do expert Lake Superior diving—including a couple of expeditions to the *Edmund Fitzgerald*.

Farnquist earned worldwide publicity when he led an

expedition to remove the ship's bell from the sunken *Fitzgerald*. Now on display at the museum, the bell has the names of all the drowned crew members engraved on it, and has become the focal point of an annual memorial service for surviving families. This annual Nov. 10 service draws a large crowd of survivors from around the country, including a large contingent of Paradise area folks whose lives have been touched by the Fitzgerald tragedy.

"Lake Superior is 1,333 feet deep, 400 miles long and 160 miles wide. There are many shipwrecks yet unexplored and even unknown," Farnquist said. "We have purchased an underwater remote-operated submarine that is capable of going down 1,500 feet to film, and even pick up, objects. It will become the single most important piece of equipment in our effort to explore and preserve our Great Lakes wrecks," he said.

Current projects include restoring the old lighthouse keeper's home, and adding a gift shop and restrooms.

Farnquist and his employees were proud to receive the 1999 Governor's Award for Arts and Culture.

"We also won a big award for our web site. People can access it at www.shipwreckmuseum.com," Farnquist said.

Stay In Your Seats

July/August 2001

Be patient with me for a few paragraphs because the conclusion of this column has had a very big impact in my life and it may have the same in yours.

I was cleaning out an old file in my office last June when I came upon an old, yellowed newspaper clipping—a column I wrote for the *Lansing State Journal* nearly 20 years ago. The column explained why I had not thrown my writings into the controversy on the wearing of seat belts—a hot issue in those days, before it was law.

Before I get to the real point of today's column, I want to reprint a portion of that old column I wrote nearly 20 years ago. It read, in part:

That subject has been avoided for two reasons. First, I don't like to bore readers with a columnist's pompous preachings for or against something. Secondly, I always subscribed to that freedom-of-choice argument that says the government ought to quit protecting people from themselves. Helmet and seat belt use is up to the individual, I've always said.

On long trips, I usually buckled my seat belt. Otherwise, I did not. Then, some of my friends—many of them policemen—began to get on my case. Bob Zuker (Zuker Tire Company) was on the phone urging me to wear seat belts. Dan Poorman, *State Journal* police reporter, ordered me to buckle my seat belt when in his car. I didn't fight back, but I sure felt nagged.

Tuesday, I had lunch with Bill Carter, director of the Lansing Area Safety Council. I stepped into Bill's car in front of the newspaper office. "Buckle your seat belt," Bill said. I told him where to get off. I said I was sick of all the nagging on that subject. We had lunch and we debated the subject.

After lunch, we were headed back when Bill said: "Jim, I want to make a stop at the Safety Council office. Come on in a minute." I soon found myself being shoved into a conference room.

"Sit down, damn you. I want you to see a short movie because I treasure you as a friend. Just sit there and shut up," he said.

The movie started. What I expected was a bloody, messy bunch of ugly auto crash scenes and some preaching on safety belts.

I saw none of that. It was simply a quiet lecture by former State Police Trooper Jack Ware. Jack told of some fatal accidents he policed during his career. He made the film's title, "Room to Live," a strong argument. The film won an international award at the National Safety Congress.

It ought to get an Academy Award. It was the most powerful, emotional 29 minutes of movie watching I ever experienced.

I won't try to tell it here. I couldn't do it justice. Let's just say that Bill Carter heard the "click" of my seat belt when I got into his car for the return trip. He didn't smile or gloat about it. He simply said: "Thanks, Jim." I should have been thanking him. I'll be buckling my seat belt in the future.

More than 50,000 persons are killed in auto accidents in the U.S. each year. Cops policing those crashes believe that thousands of persons would have survived if they had been wearing seat belts. Inside those mangled cars there is "Room to Live." The number one killer in those crashes came from being thrown from the car or into the windshield.

One person is injured in a Michigan traffic accident every one minute and 51 seconds. One in every 68 persons living in this state was injured in a car accident last year.

More than 1,300 were killed in our state, and 1982 was one of our best years, about 200 deaths fewer than normal.

Nobody says seat belts would have saved them all. But there seems no question they'd have saved many.

As the movie ended, Trooper Ware said: "In more than 23 years of policing highway accidents, I never saw a dead person unbuckled from a safety belt.

* * * * *

So, readers, as I finished reading that old column, I reflected on how I had been a seat belt zealot for so many years—constantly preaching to my son, Steve, on the subject.

As I sat there pondering that old column, the phone rang. It was my son, Steve, calling to tell me he had just survived a terrible, terrible accident. He was on his way to work from Vermontville to Lansing on Highway M-50 when he swerved to avoid a giant turtle in the roadway. A semi-truck hit Steve's little Chevy Nova head on. It threw his car into a giant spin. When it stopped, the car was crumpled into a tiny ball of wreckage. The truck left the roadway, hit a tree and rolled over.

Police at the scene could not believe both drivers survived.

"Nothing very complicated about it, Dad," Steve said. "The seat belt did it. Without it, I'd have died instantly. A seat belt also saved the truck driver."

What awful thoughts went through my mind after that phone call from my son—his wife, Susie, and their three young kids, Danny, David and Ellen. I wanted to rush down there and kiss that seat belt.

It was all the more amazing considering that Steve underwent open-heart surgery only a year ago at age 40. He survived that because of expert medical care, but an even bigger threat to his life was averted that morning in June by the simple "click" of a seat belt. Thank God.

Thanks also to an old and dear friend, Bill Carter.

Curmudgeon On Spring Break

March 2005

In a recent discussion with some friends, I expressed strong opposition to the tradition of wild college student spring breaks. One young person in the group called me an "old curmudgeon."

Wow! That hurt. I never wanted to become an old curmudgeon. Fact is, I don't think I am an old curmudgeon on the subject of college "spring-breakers" and their behavior.

Rather, for the past six years, I have become something of an expert on college spring-breakers because we have spent winters at South Padre Island, Texas, site of the biggest of all spring break gatherings of rich, spoiled, young brats who overdose on drugs and alcohol, walk around undressed in public and fall off high-rise hotel balconies to their death.

After a half-dozen such tragic deaths of spring-breakers there last March, hospital administrators and emergency room doctors made pleas to the press to get the word out to all those parents of students from colleges all over America so that they know what really goes on at spring break locations in Florida, Texas and Mexico.

Back home, mom and dad listen to the moans and groans of their college students who say they desperately need a break after long stretches of college classroom stress. So, mom and dad hand the kids their credit cards and send them off on a two-week vacation.

They arrive by the thousands and the merchants rip them off as drink prices triple and motel rates double.

Meanwhile, back home, mom and dad go to work and

worry about their budget—already vastly stretched by soaring college costs. It was mom and dad who needed that vacation in the sunny south far more than the kids.

When I was a college student, I worked full-time because my mom and dad could not afford much, even though they did all they could to help me. My dad worked long, hard hours as a milkman and a railroad worker. He came home exhausted and elevated his legs to reduce the large swelling of varicose veins. Could I have moaned about the hard life in college?

Those of us who put up with the spring break phenomenon each year at South Padre Island see a majority of the kids tossing beer bottles in the streets, urinating in public, and going around nude. My wife, Darl, and I were on the beach surf fishing one day with friends Ray and Janice Drake when a pickup truck, loaded in back with young spring breakers, came by with the horn sounding. We looked up to see a girl proudly holding up her T-shirt to show off her breasts. Later, when the truck returned with the same show, I tried to stop them. They drove on. "What were you going to do if they stopped?" Ray asked. "Well, Ray, I just had an uncontrolled urge to ask the young lady if her mother would be proud of her," I answered.

Maybe I am an old curmudgeon.

There is another side of it all, of course. College is stressful and a spring break from all that is often needed. It is also true that thousands of college students go home to help mom and dad or work at a part-time job. And many thousands go on spring break trips to help build a church or school in some troubled spot in the world.

When I was a daily columnist for the *Lansing State Journal*, I received a copy of a letter a mother wrote to her son who was graduating from college. It tells how it ought to be between a student and parent.

The mother, a single parent who made great sacrifices for her son, felt she could only give him her real feelings in writing. She sent the following to my column:

"An open letter to my son:

It has always been easier for me to put down on paper what I feel in my heart than to come out and say it.

You have just traveled a long, difficult road, which I know also has been challenging and rewarding. As I sit here alone with my thoughts, I remember the talks we had about your dreams and hopes for the future and the times you were discouraged, but determined, as day blended into night and you studied the clock around. I remember the times you would withdraw from reality out of sheer exhaustion. I saw the pain in your eyes, and longed to kiss all the hurt away as I did when you were a little boy. But you are now a man, and the struggle is yours alone. I remember also the times you would finally give in and crawl into your dorm hide-a-way, to sleep away that exhaustion.

I watched you striving to achieve your goal. You have sacrificed much and, in so doing, have accomplished much. You very soon will be going on to even bigger and better things.

It is with a heart overflowing with love and pride that I thank God that out of all the mothers in the world, he saw fit to make me yours. I pray you will never take for granted your God-given capabilities. Remember, along with privileges comes responsibility. God bless you in a very special way, my son."

Special People

Mattresses To Islands

January/February 1995

Skeptics snicker when they hear a friend of mine say he intends to move a two-story Victorian home from Mecosta to Mackinac Island.

Not me. When Wild Bill Gannon says he'll do something, he will.

Gannon, best known as "the Mattress King of Lansing" and owner of Wild Bill's Bedding, is also a Hawaii land developer and owner of three radio stations in Michigan. I've had a closeup view of his ambition and resourcefulness for more than 20 years. Yes, skeptics, he will move that monstrous and aged Victorian home all the way from Mecosta to Mackinac Island. I'm not sure how, but he'll do it.

Gannon, 47, was born in the Upper Peninsula near Channing and Crystal Falls, the son of a Michigan conservation officer. When his father was transferred to Mecosta County around 1950, the family bought an old Victorian home. Years later, Bill and his wife, Marty, made it their home when they operated furniture and bedding businesses in Lansing and Big Rapids.

"It occurred to me about a year ago," Bill said, "that our old home, worth about $100,000 at Mecosta, would be worth more than a million dollars on Mackinac Island." But it is far more than a money motive. "Somehow, our old home belongs on Mackinac Island and Marty and I would like to live there in retirement."

Gannon already has a deal with an Italian building expert who can separate the home's two stories for moving and re-connect them on the Island. He has a mover who can haul the home from Mecosta to Ludington, where it can be placed on a giant barge and hauled to the Island.

"That's the part still giving us trouble," he said. "When we get it to the island, we have a piece of property picked out for it, but moving the home from the barge to the homesite is tough. They won't let us cut down trees along the narrow roads of the island. We have looked into giant helicopters and so much more. We had a great plan to move the home down the island's airport runway to the site but that entails so much federal and state red tape that is wears you out. The airport route is still on the burner though, and we have several other alternatives. We'll work it out somehow, someday," he said.

Working things out has become a Bill and Marty Gannon specialty. Both are Michigan State University grads. Marty studied accounting and retailing while Bill studied communications, business and construction.

"I had to work my way through college," Bill said, "so I took a job as night manager of a Burger King, and that's where I met Marty, one of my employees. That was the best thing that ever happened to me in all my life."

Before college graduation, Bill bought old homes to refurbish and rent to college students. He also became foreman for Wickes Lumber Company.

"I learned an early lesson about business. You can't do much with an equity grown in home and land ownership unless you have a cash flow. I was flat broke and trying in vain to make it in the real estate and used furniture business when I made a deal with a Lansing man to rent an old building, provided I could get the first three months rent-free. That launched us into the bedding business, and the rest is history," Bill said.

Bill and Marty had a plan. Instead of working 40 hours a week and retiring after 40 years, they decided they'd work 80 hours a week and retire after 20 years.

"We missed our goal by two years," Marty said. They retired from the bedding business one year ago.

Gannon became "the mattress king" through imaginative advertising and careful attention to quality and service. His radio and TV ads told rich folks they could buy mattresses from his modest-looking store without their neighbors knowing.

"I offered midnight deliveries to their homes in Wild Bill's unmarked truck. I also offered secret parking at the rear of my store where they could enter the back door and put a paper bag over their heads and come in anonymously to shop for a low-priced mattress," he said.

When they visited us for an overnight stay in our home in Paradise, I chided Bill about his version of retirement. I reminded him that he recently bought three radio stations at Grayling and made monstrous investments in Hawaii.

"Well, Jim, the radio stations are great fun. We began with the purchase of WGRY, a small AM station. The we added the FM, and recently bought a third station, WQON-FM. It's a blast. We love the radio business," he said.

As for Hawaii, let Marty tell it.

"Bill can't stand a road he has not explored," she said. "After working ourselves nearly to death for so long, I made him take me to Hawaii in 1978. He rented a car and began exploring every corner of the island of Maui. We got on a very remote road in wild country when suddenly a pickup truck skidded to a stop crossways in the road to block our way. A dangerous-looking hippie-type guy jumped out of the truck and demanded to know what we were doing there. Bill, scared to death, tried a little white lie and said he was looking for property to purchase and had an appointment to see a realtor in the area. To make a long story short, the man took us to meet a guy who showed us some land—a very large parcel including some of the most beautiful ocean beach in the world. They said it was for sale for a mere million bucks. No way did we have that kind of money, but we kept playing the game because we were frightened of the crowd.

"Before a couple of years ended, however, Bill had managed a $400,000 loan in Hawaii and a $100,000 loan in Michigan to purchase the prime property on a land contract. Last year we were offered $4 million for the land."

Stay tuned. When that Mecosta Victorian home heads for Mackinac Island, we'll let you know.

Fleeting Fame And Other Stories From The Heart

March/April 1995

I had a bittersweet emotional experience recently that I simply can't get off my mind. I hope readers won't mind too much if I share it here.

It was an honor to speak to Central Michigan University journalism and communication students, returning to my old campus and attempting to give something back, as they say. It was an emotional thing for me as I addressed those bright young people heading off into careers similar to mine.

As I began the speech, I saw an older man make his way into the room and with halting steps, make his way to the back of the room.

When the speech was done and the students' questions were winding down, only a few of us remained at the front of the room as the older gentleman came toward me.

Suddenly, he was close enough for recognition. I just stood there, tears running down my face. It was the great Dr. Gilbert Maienknecht—my hero, my mentor, a man I love and respect.

That was the sweet part of it all as I hugged him and expressed how he honored me by coming to that event. Then came the bitter part.

Not a person in that room recognized that great man, a CMU journalism institution in his own right. He created the journalism department and was its chairman until retirement eight years ago.

It was an embarrassment that I had to introduce him in his own domain.

Later, we tired to laugh at the fleeting nature of fame.

Then he told me of a recent experience along that line and I cried again—this time sad tears.

He told it this way: "I had a student here whom I had helped get a degree and then helped her get a job. She was employed at a newspaper in Lincoln, Nebraska.

"She wrote to thank me for all I had done for her. Although I have remained a resident of Mount Pleasant all these years, she did not have my address. So she sent the letter to me in care of the Central Michigan University journalism department. They returned the letter to her saying they had no address for me. That little experience was a little more than humiliating to me, Jim, it was a genuine embarrassment."

Fame is fleeting indeed. Imagine that. Gilbert Maienknecht, mentor of famed journalists all over our land—including Dick Enberg of sports broadcast fame and Dave Smith, editor for *The Wall Street Journal, Detroit Free Press* and *Ward's Auto Work* (bible of the auto industry today).

I have great, great respect for Central Michigan University but I also have some advice for it today: You folks had better create a Central Michigan University Journalism Hall of Fame and you'd better stick Dr. Gilbert Maienknecht into it. Soon, before it's too late. A big bunch of well-known journalists will be there right in the front row. His fame may be a bit fleeting on the changing campus, but it will never flee the minds of his former students. That ought to be the real measure of this great man.

* * * * *

Since we are dumping our emotions here today, I have another story or two along those lines.

An old friend sat in my living room recently and suddenly wiped away a tear.

The friend, Bruce Cornelius, is a Lansing television news executive and a sensitive human being.

Neither of us was embarrassed. We had shared tears many times together.

"I'm sorry, Jim," he said, "my tears have nothing to do with our good conversation here. It's just that I had a couple of experiences recently that I can't get out of my mind. Two indelible images keep coming back to me from that day."

Bruce went on to explain that he was leaving his church on Sunday when he came on a scene that he described this way:

"It was a very elderly couple. I'm sure they have been married for many a year. There they were, leaving the church slowly and with halting steps. She obviously suffered from emphysema and he was obviously blind. As they made their way, she led him by the arm and he carried her oxygen tank. That scene just said so much about life, love and growing old. It was both beautiful and sad. I probably won't forget that moment the rest of my life."

Now he had me in tears. After a moment, I asked about the second unusual experience he had mentioned. He told that story this way:

"It was after that experience with that old couple in front of the church. My wife, Jan, and I went to the cemetery to visit the gravesite of a loved one. As we arrived, we watched a second old couple walk with difficulty to a grave carrying two lawn chairs. They arrived at the grave, arranged the chairs, and sat down—one on each side of the grave. There, they held a conversation for a long time. And, although there were only two people present, I'm sure it was a three-way conversation. Another moment I can't ever forget," he said.

More tears on two faces in my living room on the shore of Lake Superior.

Hiller's Still The Best

September/October 1997

A reader recently asked me, "who is your favorite professional athlete?"

"John Hiller, of course," I replied.

The reader, a younger person, was puzzled. "Who's John Hiller?" he asked.

I explained that John Hiller was a relief pitcher with the Detroit Tigers who was so good at his job that he set major league game-save records that stood for more than 10 years. Hiller wanted to play baseball more than anyone in the game's history, and he proved it by returning to the mound after three heart attacks.

Nobody gave Tiger fans more thrills than he did when he'd come into the game in the ninth inning with the bases loaded and nobody out, to strike out the side.

What's more, those were the golden years of baseball–when there were fewer arrogant athletes with zillionaire salaries.

As I visited with my young reader, I recalled that John Hiller now lives in the Upper Peninsula at Iron Mountain. So, by golly, I went there to find him.

"Hi, Jim, it's great to see you. I remember a wonderful column you wrote about me late in my career when the fans booed me a little. You gave them hell for having such short memories," he said.

Thus began a wonderful afternoon with the finest professional athlete I've ever known. I was eager for John's perspective on baseball's past and future.

Reminding him that he made less than $20,000 per year

as a major leaguer in the 1970s, I asked John how he views today's monstrous salaries.

"I don't think old-timers resent it so much. What we have a problem with today is the arrogance all that money brings to the athletes. I think these young guys ought to get down on their knees and be thankful for it all instead of displaying an arrogance and some kind of idea that they deserved it.

"They also forget the importance of the fans. They insulate themselves from the guy who buys a ticket. That is the shameful thing about the modern athlete.

"Athletes today add to their millions by collecting thousands of dollars per day selling their autographs at baseball card shows. That takes the game away from the kids and makes those players prostitutes. They ought to do those things as a courtesy to the fans or a charity fundraiser," he said.

John also noted that big money changes the feeling of teamwork. "Today's players come to the park with a briefcase, a laptop computer and a copy of the *Wall Street Journal*. They leave the park after the game and go back to their office where their real passion is managing their money and not player togetherness."

All that money puts athletes into the role of entertainers, too.

"Suddenly, the press is interested in all the things they do outside of baseball and then the athletes quit talking to the press because the press prints the truth about their private lives.

"In my day, I had great relations with the press. I made myself accessible and answered their questions honestly. If I was rotten that day, I said so. The press also understood that I'd never bad-mouth a teammate, my manager or the club management."

Originally from Toronto, Hiller has been a U.S. resident since the middle '60s, when he joined the Tigers.

After four years with Detroit, he suffered three heart

attacks at age 27. After surgery and treatment, Hiller felt he was ready to go back to work in 1971.

"Tiger management was afraid I'd die on the mound in front of thousands of fans. They fought my return. I finally got an appointment with a famed heart specialist, Willard Hurst. He went to bat for me. He told the Tigers I'd have another heart attack if I didn't get back into baseball. Also, I think Billy Martin, my manager, convinced the Tigers they needed me on the mound. The Tigers cut my salary from $20,000 to $17,000 and gave me a contract," he said.

Martin called Hiller into a 1972 game at Chicago, and the rest is history. Hiller racked up his major league record of 38 saves, and by 1974 repeated that accomplishment and recorded 17 wins.

John was out of baseball several years before he was inducted into the Canadian Baseball Hall of Fame in 1985 and got the bug to return as a pitching coach.

"I told the Tiger management that I didn't want to coach players making millions of dollars so I took a job as a roving minor league pitching coach for four years. Then I developed a circulatory blockage behind my knee. Doctors think I should have my leg amputated, but I still manage some golf and gardening."

John is pleased with his coaching of the now-famed John Smoltz. "He was the Tiger's best arm in the farm system. I hated it when the Atlanta Braves manager asked about Smoltz in a proposed trade. I told him Smoltz was the best the Tigers had in the minors. He was a great kid to coach and he says I helped him a lot. I feel good about that," he said.

In between all that, John tried farming near the tiny U.P. town of Felch. "It was a disaster. I ran out of money and had to go back to work," he laughed.

Hiller still goes back to Detroit to help with charity events for kids, but he hates to leave his Iron Mountain digs. For perspective on that, I sought out his friend and golfing partner, Mick Simone.

"John loves it here where few know he is a baseball celebrity," Simone said.

When I asked John why he chose the U.P., he grinned and said: "You know why us Yoopers do that. This country is still civilized. I don't lock my house or my car. Come to think of it, I left my billfold on the car seat. It's safe there."

John Hiller was the best on the field, and he's the best off the field, too.

The Gold Crown Mystery

November/December 1997

Whenever I see my doctor, John Neuman, I ask him to open his mouth and say "ahhh."

Although John is a longtime close friend, he never laughs at that. Fact is he gets a little irritated. My little stunt brings back a memory he'd like to forget.

So, I think it's time for a column—a kind of investigative report on "Whatever Happened to John's Gold Crown?"

It began about 10 years ago when John and I were together for a day and I noticed he kept pushing his tongue around in his mouth.

"What's wrong in your mouth?" I asked.

"Nothing," he snapped, obviously eager to be off the subject.

But I persisted, as a good reporter should. I finally pieced it all together—interrogating John, his wife, Carol, and the good doctor's office staff.

It seems John had lost his gold crown. He searched his office, home, garden, car and everywhere. Then it occurred to Doc that he might have swallowed it. He secretly slinked off to St. Lawrence Hospital's X-ray department where he asked for a picture of his stomach and intestines.

Sure enough! There it was.

John studied the X-Ray carefully and began a series of calculations. He figured the gold crown was about one day away from emergence.

It all reminded me of the time when my brother, Don, swallowed a penny. We had outdoor plumbing in those days and my mom wanted to make sure the penny had passed through. So she made Don use a "thundermug" inside the house. How I remember that morning years ago when we all heard the "plink" of the penny as it struck the bottom of the thundermug.

Thus I wondered if Doc Neuman's gold crown went "plink" or "plunk" when it hit his thundermug. I'm sure he used one. After all, there was about $200 worth of gold in that crown.

I told John I'd check to see if his mouth was back to normal the next time I saw him. I told him I'd then check with his dentist to see if he had a new gold crown installed. If not, I said, we'd all know what happened to the old one.

I told John the whole episode would make a great subject for a newspaper column.

"I'm not worried, Jim," he said. "No writer, especially one of your diminished talent, could clean up a story like that to make supper time reading in a family newspaper," Neuman said.

After 10 years of hard and intense investigative reporting, I've been unable to find any dental or medical evidence of a new gold crown installation in John. And yet, he has a gold crown.

Some columns are harder to write than others.

Mr. Baseball Writes A Book

July/August 1998

Country Lines readers will recall the great George Kell because his picture has graced the cover of this magazine in his role as a supporter of rural electric cooperatives. Eclipsing all of that, of course, is Kell's fame as the Hall of Fame/Detroit Tigers third baseman—some think the best in baseball history.

So, what puts words about George Kell under my byline again today? Well, as many of you know, George and I are longtime friends. He wrote me recently to tell of a new, exciting chapter in his already amazing life. He has written a book called: *"Hello, Everybody, I'm George Kell."* Those words opened thousands of Detroit Tiger broadcasts until he retired from the broadcast booth a couple of years ago.

You don't have to be a baseball fan to love and respect Kell. His classy posture off the baseball field equals the days on the field when he beat out Ted Williams for the batting title.

George's letter said, in part: "Time is running out for old friends, and we must meet soon for a good hug and conversation. I have just gone off the deep end, Jim, and have done what I said I'd never do. I wrote a book with the help of another of your old friends, Dan Ewald (former Grand Rapids sports writer and Detroit Tigers' publicist for 18 years). I will be doing book signings and the Tigers are planning a George Kell Day at the old stadium. I'm deeply honored. I am sending you a personal copy of the book along with a recorded version I have read onto tape."

I can't wait to get that stuff. What fun it will be to relive those years with my baseball hero and friend.

When Kell broke in with the old Philadelphia Athletics, in 1943, never did he think he had just embarked on a 53-year major league ride from induction into baseball's Hall of Fame to an equally accomplished baseball broadcasting career. Kell has experienced changes in the national pastime that few could imagine.

So many landmarks. He is one of a few remaining players who were managed by the legendary Connie Mack, and played during and after the war years. He was there as a player when baseball broke the color barrier. But mainly, he was a star during baseball's golden years—a period most observers feel was the greatest in baseball history.

Following his playing days, Kell moved up to the television booth for a 38-year run. How many millions of us spent summer nights listening to the inimitable voice of George Kell. How we all loved the down-home insights of this man.

In 1949, Kell beat Ted Williams by one point to win the American league batting title. He also called several World Series' and he even turned down an offer to manage the Detroit Tigers.

As great as all that is my admiration for Kell goes outside his professional life. Despite all that fame, he remains an Arkansas good ol' boy, still making his home in Swifton, where he was born and spent his entire life. He is still a leader in the same church where his father was a leader before him. He has lived in the same house since he won the batting title some 50 years ago.

Stories of all that—in Kell's own words—will surely be a special book on my shelf.

I recall some years ago when George was inducted into the Baseball Hall of Fame. I asked him what was the first thing he did when he got the news.

"I was in a motel. I was so excited on the phone that I couldn't even take notes," Kell said. "I jumped right on a plane to go home to Swifton to personally take that news to my father who was lying there in a nursing home bed. I watched tears of joy flow down his face and that, Jim, was the greatest thrill of my baseball career."

Somewhere in the 1970s, my Grand Ole Opry friend, Whisperin' Bill Anderson, wrote of the day: "Where Have All Our Heroes Gone?" I recalled that I wrote Bill to say at least one hero remained—George Kell. Young athletes today need a better understanding of what makes a hero. It's not always the grand slam or a no-hitter.

As Ed Howe once said: "A boy does not have to go off to war to become a hero. He can say he doesn't like pie when he sees there is not enough to go around."

Mentioning Bill Anderson and George Kell in the same paragraph reminds me of the day I received a phone call from Bill Anderson telling me of the great thrill he had in meeting George Kell in a parking lot at the Nashville, Tennessee, airport.

"I couldn't believe it," Bill said, "there I was visiting with that fantastic man. He even signed a baseball for my son and we talked about you for a long time."

Later that same day, I got another phone call. This time it was Kell. "My God, Jim, you won't believe it. I got to meet Bill Anderson. What a thrill it was for me. He even gave me a ride from the Nashville airport to my hotel. We talked about you. My admiration for him and his music is equal to yours."

It is a special vicarious pleasure when two of your heroes meet for a warm handshake.

Reader Magic

September/October 2000

The year 2000 brought me many high honors and a huge guilt trip.

It all began in January, when the *Lansing State Journal* named me among the 100 most influential people in Lansing's last 100 years. Wow, Jim Hough listed there with the guy who invented the Oldsmobile!

Then came the April induction to the Michigan Journalism Hall of Fame—a big banquet attended by about 500 of the big shooters in the world of journalism. Wow again. A high perch for an old Upper Peninsula stump jumper. Then came May and the big, annual Michigan Parade in Lansing. This year's theme was "honoring our own" and I was named a parade co-marshal with Magic Johnson and Mohammed Ali. Wow again.

Then the Michigan State Senate interrupted a session to honor me on the Senate floor. They asked me to speak to the Senate with my family gathered at the podium. An emotional moment and a big honor.

So, where's the guilt trip in all of this? Well, it's time I made a confession to readers.

My guilt trip came because they were honoring me for things my readers did. No, come on now, this is not a case of false modesty. It is the truth. Let me make my case.

They cited many, many accomplishments in the more than 8,000 columns I wrote for the *Lansing State Journal* and *Country Lines*. Let me explain why all those accomplishments were not mine.

It didn't take much for me to interview an old burro at

Lansing's Potter Park Zoo. Herman, the beloved burro, was a Zoo favorite and he called for the formation of a Friends Of The Zoo Society. Readers jumped in great numbers and the organization was formed. Six months later, it had 3,000 members and it has raised millions to support the Zoo in the past 20 years. In Lansing, they call me "The Father of the Zoo." Imagine that—all because of what some readers did.

I interviewed Herman again and quoted him as saying the Zoo needed a baby elephant. Area kids then went door-to-door selling Herman buttons at 50 cents each until they had $5,000 to buy a baby elephant. My column got credit for that, too. And so it went with other special exhibits. I'm darned proud of that Zoo today, but it was built by my readers, not me.

I wrote columns about barriers to people with physical handicaps, especially those who are blind and in wheelchairs. Michigan legislators read those columns and responded with laws that created curb cuts for wheelchairs, braille markings in elevators, and more. Result: A presidential citation from Richard M. Nixon for service to the handicapped. It was presented to me by former Gov. G. Mennen Williams at a big banquet in Lansing. I was honored, of course, but we all know that was the work of my readers.

During the Vietnam War, I received a letter from a Lansing soldier suggesting that unpopped popcorn was a good Christmas gift because they couldn't get that over there. The owner of a popcorn company read the column and brought me a ton of popcorn. Junior high students and service clubs joined in to put the popcorn into two-pound packages addressed to Michigan servicemen in Vietnam. They had so much fun that they did it again the next year. My column got the credit for all that. Ridiculous.

An old man, R.J. Scheffel, was my neighbor. He got bored in retirement, so he went to his workshop and built some scooters and wheelbarrows for some kids whose parents could not afford toys at Christmas. I wrote about it and mentioned that he could use some donated building materials. Suddenly, materials came by the truckload and, just as suddenly, the "R. J. Scheffel Christmas Workshop" was filled with other old-timers with carpentry skills. For over 20 years, they have produced thousands of toys annually for needy kids. The Hall of Fame people credited me for all that, too. But you see what I mean.

I could go on and on with this. The point is that a newspaper's power is in its readers—not its publishers, editors, reporters, and columnists. Readers talk of how I got into their lives, but they need to know how much they got into my life. I spilled a lot of tears on my typewriter over the years, tears of sadness and tears of joy.

When a 4-year-old girl, Alicia Rouse, had to have her leg amputated, I cried all over my typewriter all day. I wrote about her and readers filled her hospital room with stuffed animals and tons of mail. They—the readers—made a difference. Several months later, Alicia walked up to my desk on artificial legs to thank me. I cried again, and I wanted every one of those readers to be standing there with me.

At the Hall of Fame ceremonies, they said my column got into the lives of the readers. But think of how the readers got into my life. I wish readers could have been there with me this past June, 14 years after the amputations of Alicia's legs. I watched her stand tall on artificial legs as she graduated from Gaylord High School. She was even captain of the swim team. This time, Alicia and I cried together. I'll be there at her wedding, too. Thanks, readers. You played a very big part in Alicia's life.

Now, all these years later, I wish every one of those readers could stand next to me on my high perch in the Michigan Journalism Hall of Fame.

Much has also been made of my blindness during my career. It is true that I have not been able to read the newspaper or drive a car for about 40 years, but there is another side to that, too.

My all-time favorite writer was the great Helen Keller. She was born in the early 1900s, and she was blind, deaf and unable to speak. But she fought off her handicap and began a writing career. She became world famous. She was the guest of kings and she was loved by commoners. Just before her death, she wrote: "Thank you God for my handicap, for through it I found myself and my work." Maybe just a little bit of that fits Jim Hough.

Thanks readers—I love you, every one.

Mr. Parker's Legacy

November/December 2000

Many honors came my way in the year 2000, but the biggest honor of all was one I did not want. I hated it. I detested it. It put me in tears.

That biggest of all honors came in September when I was called to the bedside of Karl Parker, 86, my old high school coach.

When I got there, I found myself standing by that bedside with an old friend, Jim Mills. We are both in our late 60s, but we still call him "Mr. Parker."

"Listen, men," he said, "I hate to ask it of you but I am going to die soon and I'd like to ask you two old athletes and friends to speak at my funeral."

Mills, a retired Newberry banker, and this retired newspaper columnist lost it. That was too much. We love Mr. Parker so much.

"Now listen, you guys," Parker said, "I know that is tough and I don't want you to do a big eulogy and praise for your old coach. I just want you to represent all those former athletes and students I had. Get tough now, both of you, and go up there and get one more base hit for the old coach."

At the time of this writing, Mr. Parker still lives, in severe pain in a battle with cancer. What an enormous honor it is to have him think of us that way.

Mr. Parker is an Upper Peninsula legend. He led Brimley High School to state Class D basketball championships in 1950 and 1951. He is in the Michigan Coaches Hall of Fame, the Upper Peninsula Sports Hall of Fame and the Brimley High School Sports Hall of Fame. He is so loved by so many even after his long teaching and coaching service at Brimley and Newberry. The list of his league championships and state tournament trophies is long.

On many occasions, I have been a speaker at Brimley High School commencements and reunions. My first two words from the podium were always "Karl Parker." Those two words never failed to bring a standing ovation of several minutes.

He was everyone's favorite teacher—after they graduated. Many, however, hated him in school because he was a tough, tough teacher. He demanded that each do their best whether it was on the athletic field or in his English, algebra or history classes.

But it was his fairness and concern for the individual that drew the most admiration. Gerald Brehm, a retired Detroit Police Department detective-sergeant, put it best: "I was not a great athlete or a great student at Brimley, but Mr. Parker always made me feel I was as good as any other kid in school. He gave me confidence in life that I might not otherwise have had."

Mills, the first student inductee to the Brimley Sports Hall of Fame, claims he was the luckiest of all Parker's former athletes. "He caused me to excel in all sports for four years of high school. But for so many, many years in later life, we were friends and golf partners at Newberry where he was still teaching me, even as Jim Hough and I stood by his bedside that day in September," Mills says.

Mr. Parker had a passion for giving back what the community gave to him and his family. Whenever he was congratulated for his 20 years of service on the Newberry Board of Education or so many other community services, he always responded with his favorite quote from the Bible: "To whom much is given, much is expected." One of my favorite quotes sure fits Mr. Parker. Ralph Waldo Emerson said, "To be respected, a man must respect."

All of Mr. Parker's former athletes have a story to tell in

which he had great impact on their lives. My story involves the day we beat the Sault Ste. Marie baseball team for the first time ever. I was a freshman and the team's right fielder. I could field well but I could not hit. Midway in the game, I made a diving catch of a line drive for the third out. It kept the game close. But when it came to the last inning and we had the winning runs on second and third base, I was the next scheduled hitter with two men out. I didn't even go to the on-deck circle because Mr. Parker had several better hitters on the bench and, in that situation, would normally pinch hit for me. But he came to the bench, took me by the arm and led me away from the other players to make a little speech I have never forgotten: "Jimmy, you are a good hitter. It's just that you don't know it. This game is all about confidence. It was your great catch that got us here today and I'm not going to substitute for you. Go up there and get me a base hit. But listen, son, if you can't get it done, I'll love you for trying."

Cy Young himself couldn't have gotten me out at the moment. I smashed a single past the pitcher's ear and we whipped 'em. But there was no carrying me off the field. I ran to hug Mr. Parker. It was his base hit, not mine. From that moment on, I was ready to tackle the world. Now, in later years, what I think about most is that Mr. Parker in that moment cared more about raising a kid than he did about winning a baseball game.

Jim Mills was the third baseman on that team so many years ago. The more I think about it, we will do OK at your funeral, Mr. Parker, because you made us tough.

Cops Know How To Lend A Hand

October 2001

Recently, I listened to a young policeman moaning the blues about how difficult it is today to be a cop. Much of his complaint fell on my deaf ears.

While I admit a police officer's job has never been easy and that it takes a special dedication to do such work, I think today's cops have no idea what it was like in the 1960s and 1970s—the days when police officers across our land were called "pigs."

What makes me an authority on all that?

Well, I was a daily columnist for the *Lansing State Journal* in those days and I was always troubled by the bad image given to so many hard-working, dedicated cops. They were always on the front pages of the newspapers and the lead story of TV news—wearing their riot helmets and doing battle with all those protesters. Usually, the scene was a college campus where young people burned their draft cards and the American flag.

Many of my close friends were cops in those days and it saddened me that the public never got to see their other side—full of love, warmth and concern for the safety of their neighbors.

So, I used my column to make something positive out of it all. Somebody came up with an idea for an annual football game to be called the "Pigs and Freaks Bowl." It became a big annual event at Michigan State University's Spartan Stadium, with all proceeds going to St. Jude Children's Hospital. One year, the stadium was almost a sellout and the event raised up to $40,000 per year. Hidden under those helmets were the clean-cut hairdos of the cops and the long hair and beards of the "freaks." What was revealed to all of us, however, was what each side had in common.

My column continued to befriend the cops over the years. I was made an honorary lifetime member of the Central Michigan Law Enforcement Association, and the Michigan State Police made up a special identification card certifying me as an honorary Michigan State Police trooper. They say it is the only such ID card ever issued.

When I retired from my newspaper job in 1986, more than 1,000 people attended a banquet held at the Lansing Civic Arena. I don't mention that here to brag but because it gives me a chance to say that, by actual count, there were nearly 200 cops in that audience. They appreciated it when someone took the trouble to look behind the badge.

Because they are little understood by the public, cops often turn inside for their close friends and social life. Thus, I have always been honored to be invited to join them at many social gatherings and fishing trips where I was the only non-cop.

About 30 years ago, a group of Lansing area cops got tired of meeting at funerals and decided to start an organization called the "Keystone Cops." The aim was an annual lunch in the Christmas season. It always draws nearly 300 cops, both working and retired. The program was always presented by the late Rev. Father Jerome McEachin and I was the master of ceremonies. Fr. Mac became ill about 20 years ago and I had to fill in. Thus, I have been the annual speaker at that event for about 20 years. What an honor it is. They are among this nation's finest and they have lived through troubled professional and personal times that should make the modern young cop blush.

I fear my next appearance at the Keystone Cops podium will be my hardest yet. One of my closest friends, retired State Police Trooper Ed Busch, died of a heart attack while on a fishing trip in Canada. Ed and I attended that Keystone Cops luncheon together for the past 15 years. How I will miss him there. We were like brothers.

In a way, Ed Busch was typical of all those cops I have tried to describe here. He was a little-known policeman who gave the taxpayers a great effort every day for 30 years. Underneath that big bulk was the softest heart, and I could tell you hundreds of warm stories about him.

In his later professional years, he was a fingerprint expert for the State Police Crime Lab in East Lansing. And, because of my vision problems, I usually took a city bus home from work each day. Often, Ed would call to say he would stop by to give me a ride home. With no words spoken, he often turned left on M-99 and headed to a nursing home in Dimondale. That's where my father lived in a battle with Alzheimer's disease. Ed would sit in the parking lot while I visited my dad. I always came out of that building in tears, but when Ed's big arm hugged my shoulder, I was soon okay. What a man.

Like Ed, most cops don't make big news. They just plod along doing great things for the American public every day.

I recall when a 13-year-old girl was raped and murdered west of Charlotte. The cops knew who had committed the crime but the efforts of several police agencies could not develop evidence to prove it. Ed, with a 13-year-old daughter of his own, was terribly troubled by all that. I called Ed's boss, Lt. George Hein, and asked him to send Ed to that crime scene. Reluctantly, George did that as a favor to me. In one afternoon, Ed Busch lifted that little girl's handprint off the hatchback of the suspect's car. He's in jail yet today, right where he was sent, only by the great work of a great cop.

We will have a silent prayer for Ed at the next Keystone Cops luncheon.

Songs In The Key Of Success

November/December 2001

I just listened to a recording by a very famous singer. It sent my memories back more than 30 years. So, I thought I'd turn to my typewriter and do my Paul Harvey imitation of "the rest of the story."

It was in the mid-1960s and I was a young columnist for the *Lansing State Journal*. There was a young lad from the Saginaw area who was getting a lot of attention as a musician and as a student at the Michigan School For The Blind in Lansing.

So I went to visit the lad, who was then about 16. We sat together on a park bench on the school campus.

The lad, totally blind, seemed a bit sad to me. I asked if he was unhappy. "Yes, Mr. Hough, I guess I am a little unhappy," he said. "I have a great opportunity with Motown Records to travel and become a successful musician, but I can't leave high school. They say the law insists I stay here at school, unless I have a full-time tutor to travel with me."

I wrote a column about him and it brought a response from a Lansing area man, Ted Hull, a school teacher who had become blind. Soon, we had Ted and the young blind musician teamed up and they went on the road for Motown Records.

But you know the rest of the story. Stevie Wonder has become the most awarded musician in America's history. Back in those days, he made regular appearances on the Ed Sullivan Show. His vocals and harmonica recordings were always at the top of the music charts.

Soon, Stevie was graduating from the School For The

Blind and he asked the superintendent, Dr. Robert Thompson, to "please get Mr. Hough to be our commencement speaker." It was an honor then, of course, but it became a much bigger honor as the years passed and as Stevie became more than a great musician. He has remained a classy person.

Bruce Cornelius, a *Lansing State Journal* photographer, shot a great picture when they handed Stevie that diploma. It was printed large on the front page of the newspaper. Nobody has ever seen a bigger and more prideful smile.

Shortly before that graduation ceremony, I saw Stevie perform "Alphie" with his harmonica on the Ed Sullivan Show.

I told Stevie that night how much I enjoyed "Alphie." Soon, I received a record album in the mail. The cover called it "EIVETS REDNOW"—Stevie Wonder spelled backwards. The lead song on the album was "Alphie." Wow.

Our paths have not crossed again in all those years and I don't know if Stevie would remember me. But I can never forget him.

It is, indeed, ironic that I became legally blind about the time Stevie graduated from that school in Lansing.

It still amazes me when so many well-meaning people with normal sight express such shock that a blind person could have such a successful career. Stevie's talent and work ethic was nurtured by the late Jack Chard, a blind music teacher at the school and by Hull, a blind teacher of academics.

I don't know why, but none of that has ever amazed me. I guess I have been blessed to know and work with some very great and talented people who suffer severe handicaps. One experience in that regard has stayed with me. I was asked to be a speaker at the Grand Rapids Amway Hotel for a convention of the American Council For The Blind. About 2,000 blind persons from all over the country came there. I met doctors, lawyers, judges, teachers and business people. Each a success story.

My wife, Darl, still talks of the time we left our hotel room there and got on the elevator with eight leader dogs—all being led outside to do their duty in a designated part of the hotel parking lot.

And I have had the privilege to meet a couple of other blind heroes in the music business—Ray Charles and Ronnie Milsap. Recently, I listened to a National Public Radio interview with Ray Charles. I can't recall the exact quote but Ray said something like this: "No, no, no, I don't have bitterness about my blindness. I have had a great life and I have done everything I ever wanted to do. I am blessed and I am grateful."

And so it is with all handicapped people who shrug it all off and get on with their lives. A great lesson for many "normal" people I know.

If I knew how to reach Stevie by phone, my first words would be a line from one of his great hits: "I just called to say I love you."

Readers Have Heart

September 2003

Most of us have a favorite writer and many of us comment on how that writer gets into our life.

But I wonder how many readers realize all the ways they get into the life of the writer. So, this column today is not about this writer. It is about you, the reader. I will try to explain reader impact on me.

Last fall, doctors diagnosed me with cancer of the lymph glands. Since then, I have lived with such disturbing words as "cancer" and "biopsy," and I have undergone two surgeries and many weeks of radiation. It was heavy stuff for me and my family, even though I have a low-grade lymphoma and the prognosis for long-term remission is considered good.

Now let me tell you how readers fit into all that. As many of you know, I wrote a daily column in the *Lansing State Journal* for nearly 30 years until my retirement 15 years ago. The writer who replaced me, John Schneider, is a longtime friend. So, John recently wrote a few paragraphs telling readers of that column about my illness and urged them to drop me a line of encouragement.

Wow! We received more than 300 letters. My-oh-my, how those readers got into my life. My daily trips to the mailbox were exciting for weeks. As many of you know, I have been legally blind for some 40 years, and my wife, Darl, has to read to me. On many occasions during those readings I had to leave to take a walk outside, where I wiped away tears. So many of those letters came from strangers. Readers told of the ways I had gotten into their lives as a writer.

They told of success stories in beating cancer and they

offered their prayers and good wishes.

When I retired from the *Lansing State Journal*, the publisher asked me to describe my readers with one word. I quickly replied "heart." And so, that description still fits, even with John Schneider's readers today. It says so much about the real nature and real warmth of people in our land. In my days as a columnist, I was often amazed at what readers did. I suggested we improve Lansing's Potter Park Zoo, and readers jumped to raise about $2 million. I asked readers to demand that our legislators create laws to help people with handicaps. That brought me a Presidential Citation. And so it went. At the end of that career, I wound up in the Michigan Journalism Hall of Fame. For me, however, there was never a doubt: it was readers with heart who put me there.

After all these years, readers with heart are still doing great things for me. We have this lymphoma thing under control and face a better future, in no small measure, because of the encouragement, prayers and good wishes of readers.

I have saved every one of those letters and I have answered nearly 100 of them. I wish there was space here to reprint many of them. One person wrote to say she had cancer as a child and I wrote a column asking readers to cheer her up. They sent her hundreds of letters and gifts. In her letter, she said, "Now, Mr. Hough, I am 39 years old and I am returning the favor."

Alicia Rouse, a college student at Traverse City, wrote to say her grandfather in Lansing had sent her a clipping from Schneider's column and she wanted to come and visit me. That letter really put me in tears because I recalled the time about 20 years ago when little Alicia suffered from a rare blood disease that forced the amputation of both her legs. I told readers about it and they filled her hospital room with letters, cards, stuffed animals and money.

About a year later, I looked up from my typewriter in the newsroom to see a little girl walking to my desk on halting legs. "Hi, Mr. Hough, I am Alicia Rouse and I told my mom I wanted to come and see you with my new legs." So much for tough, cynical old reporters. There was not a dry eye in the newsroom. My, how that little girl got into a writer's life. When she graduated from high school, Darl and I were there. We will be there when she gets married and when she graduates from college.

And so, life between a writer and readers goes on. But it is not as one-way as you might think. None of us knows what will be dealt to us in life or whether we will get to see grandchildren graduate from school. But one thing is for sure: *As long as I live, I will never forget readers who turned to my byline.* Your heart lets us share a real and pure love. Thanks.

Seatbelt Trivia

October 2003

Michigan residents have reason to be very proud as the "click it or ticket" enforcement of seatbelt laws is now nationwide.

But a little-known fact is that a Michigan man, the late Glen Sheren, invented seatbelts back in 1941.

For so many years, most of us resisted buckling up and state legislatures found the subject controversial. Now, more than 60 years after Glen's invention, every state but New Hampshire has seatbelt laws. The National Traffic Safety Agency and the National Transportation Department have launched a campaign to levy $100 fines for failure to comply. That's good news because the lifesaving aspect of seatbelts has long been documented.

Glen Sheren's patent on seatbelts was little-known about 25 years ago when I uncovered it in a column I wrote for the *Lansing State Journal*. A Michigan State Police officer asked me to start a contest on who had worn seatbelts the longest. The contest winner was a man who had worn them 31 years. But the column also uncovered Sheren's invention.

Sheren, an old pilot, was recovering from auto crash injuries when the idea came to him for seatbelts. He installed them in his 1941 Packard. He welded the units to the car doors and frame. He obtained a patent.

A major hurdle, however, was that auto manufacturers in those days considered the idea ludicrous. His first belts were marketed as Kar Belts and he manufactured them—as many as 200 per day—in a garage at his Mason home. But no car companies could be enticed. Ford and Studebaker gave him lots of encouragement but no orders. So, in 1954, Sheren sold his patent and business to Spartan Automotive of Jackson. Two years later, that company went out of business.

By 1960, there were 70 companies in America making auto safety belts and Sheren joined a long list of inventors who were ahead of their time.

He made only a modest profit from the invention. Throughout most of his life, he sold and serviced cars in the Lansing area and his inventions were a sideline.

Two of his other inventions, Filter Flow, which allows firefighters to draw water from debris-filled streams, and Circle Air, which dries fire hoses, are still in production today.

Just think how famous Glen Sheren would be in America today if he had not sold that patent 50 years ago.

Voice Of The Soo

January 2005

It's not often when Bill Thorne, dean of Michigan radio broadcasters and voice of the Soo, asks to interview you.

But I arrived at Bill's microphone with a special plan to turn the tables on him. As he opened the interview and asked me about my induction to the Michigan Journalism Hall of Fame, I took the microphone and, to his surprise, I began my interview of the man who will begin his 57th year as a radio personality and community leader.

Soon, however, the time constraints and commercial interruptions of radio frustrated me. The show ended and I turned to my typewriter to finish the job.

Bill was 17 and a junior in high school when he decided he wanted to become a radio disc jockey. For 30 consecutive days, he went to the manager of Radio Station WSOO to ask for a job. The manager finally tired of it all and gave Bill a midnight shift as a combination disc jockey and janitor.

The rest is an inspirational history of Sault Ste. Marie radio.

Thorne, 72, has done it all. One of his regular shows, Sunday Morning Hymn Time, is in its 47th year and his popular Saturday morning show "The Four Horsemen," is in its 39th year.

Although there are several other radio stations in the area with young and vibrant "personalities," Thorne has been named the top of that heap for the past three years in a community contest sponsored by the *Sault Evening News*.

One of his proudest moments came eight years ago when he stood with cap and gown at Lake Superior State University to receive a college degree along with his granddaughter. "I'm in tears of joy and pride every time I think of that," Bill said.

While his community service and radio longevity are legend hereabouts, all that takes second fiddle to Bill's pride in his Indian heritage. His great-great grandfather, John Gurnoe, was chief of the Soo Tribe of Chippewa Indians and his teepee once stood on the St. Marys River shore at the current site of the large fountain in the Corps of Engineers Park.

And it does not end there. His great grandfather, Henry Thorne, was the captain on the Monitor, the famed ship of the Civil War.

Thorne's grandpa was also a famous fiddler and he attracted the attention of carmaker Henry Ford, who financed the production of an RCA record of his grandpa playing his own composition of 'Whitefish On the Rapids.' "Grandpa was sure proud of that," Bill said.

Bill is also proud of his cousin, Taffy Abel, the first Indian to play in the National Hockey League. "Those were the days when the Soo was a center of hockey, long before the Red Wings in Detroit," he said.

In the early days of radio, wages were small and a DJ had to have other jobs to pay the family bills.

"Multiple jobs have always been my life," Bill said. "In the early days, I was a county juvenile officer and I went across to the Canadian Soo to sign-on in the early morning at a small radio station there. Then I came back to Michigan to work all day as a juvenile officer before signing on the midnight shift as a DJ at WSOO."

Although he never interrupted his radio career, Bill has served in full-time jobs as the city's urban renewal director, assistant to a senator, and director of an organization to help the poor and elderly.

Another hat he wore in those days was a promoter of country music shows in the Soo. Among his friends were

Johnny Cash, Faron Young, Jim Reeves and Patsy Cline. He even interviewed Elvis a couple of times.

In 1959, Bill was named "DJ of the Year" by the Grand Ole Opry. In those days, there was only one such award covering all radio stations, big and small.

"That was a great honor," Bill said, "I got to perform on several national broadcasts and spend a lot of time backstage at the Opry. For me, that was like a kid in a candy store."

As part of a Michigan Week promotion 15 years ago, then Gov. Jim Blanchard asked his staff to locate the longest-serving radio broadcaster in Michigan. The buck stopped at Bill Thorne and the governor came to the Soo to present the award.

"I guess that means nobody has passed me since," Bill laughed. "I used to say I wanted to make a half-century, but now I am shooting for 60 years," he said.

All of this has special nostalgia for me because Bill is only a month older than me and I grew up listening to WSOO, a station that went on the air in 1940. It has broadcast every Detroit Tiger game since. How I remember those days as a kid—sitting there at Strongs, with my father and staring at an old Philco battery-powered radio to hear the great Harry Heilman broadcast Tiger games.

My personal compliments to WSOO, for its constant commitment to community information and betterment. Not all stations do that because they never had my friend, Bill Thorne, to lead the way.

Operation RoundUp

May/June 1997

I've had some prideful and emotional moments in the 12 years of my association with Michigan's rural electric cooperatives. But one such moment at the annual meeting of Tri-County Electric Cooperative put me in tears—tears of pride, tears that come when you are darned proud of America and its people.

I was there waiting to take the stage as the event speaker, when Richard Palermo made his annual report on the cooperative's "People Fund." Tri-County and Great Lakes Energy cooperatives are the only ones in Michigan with a People Fund in operation. [Since 1997, several other cooperatives have started similar programs.] I'm asking the rest of you to pay attention for a moment while I tell you all about a thing called "Operation Roundup."

You could see the pride and enthusiasm in the Tri-County audience that day as Palermo told them they had given more than $100,000 that year to needy families, individuals and community organizations.

"Each of you can take full credit for the $100,000, even though it only cost each co-op member about 50 cents per month," Palermo said.

Fact is, Tri-County's People Fund, now only four years

old, has already put more than $400,000 back into the area communities—each dollar going directly to enrich lives.

How does it work? Well, let's take Tri-County Electric as an example. The average member's monthly bill is $77.56. When your bill comes, your cooperative "rounds it up" to the next dollar, or $78. The extra 44 cents goes into the People Fund. Participation is optional but more than 90 percent of Tri-County's members have jumped in with enthusiasm.

Bob Matheny, Tri-County's general manger, gets a bit emotional himself when he talks about the People Fund.

"You get choked up reading the letters from families and individuals trying to say thanks, he said. "Recently I read a letter written in the very shaky hand of an elderly, arthritic woman. She thanked God for our being there to help her. I like the program because it spells community responsibility and tells the world that our organization and its people care a lot about their neighbors."

Palermo, who heads a state of Michigan unit to investigate welfare fraud, has been chairman of the Tri-County People Fund since it started.

"We are not a welfare fund and we avoid all political and governmental involvement. We help individuals and organizations to help themselves. While we make emergency grants to individuals and families, most of our funds go to community organizations," he said.

A People Fund committee, made up of well-known and responsible people from the cooperative service area, meets monthly to review requests for aid.

They have made grants to fire departments for a jaws-of-life, to an organization doing bone marrow screening for cancer patients, to a community recreation program for little league uniforms, to a community library for equipment, provided seed money for a rural community's ambulance and medical equipment, helped a family deal with a devastating illness and tragedy, and so much more.

"Food, shelter, health needs and education are the main

categories of concern in our grants," Palermo said.

People Fund programs are popular and growing in rural electric cooperatives around the United States.

The former Oceana Electric Cooperative (now part of Great Lakes Energy) distributed about $70,000 from their People Fund since it started two years ago. With their new merger with O & A Electric and the addition of 30,000 members, their People Fund may triple in the future.

Cindy Hodges, member services representative from Great Lakes Energy, said "it also brings tears to [her eyes]" to hear of the needs of families and children. "We have helped a family get a furnace in the winter and helped one get a well, so many times items out of the reach of dedicated parents in financial trouble," she said.

All the money stays in the cooperative area—none going to big cities like Lansing or Detroit. What's more, each member's contribution is tax deductible.

At that Tri-County annual meeting, I sat there next to an old friend, Jim Mull, retired Michigan State Police lieutenant and former Isabella County sheriff. He too, was a bit emotional.

"This is the greatest thing, Jim," he said, "I serve on the committee and it's a great thing people can do when they pull together, each with a tiny tug. You don't miss the few cents a month when you pay your electric bill, but you can thrill each month to see the good things done with our spare change," he said.

Look for other co-ops to start their own programs. If you'd like yours to start one, tell your board of directors. Tri-County, Great Lakes and Cherryland will be glad to offer advice.

First Light Was Magical

September/October 1998

It was a moment in my life 57 years ago that I can never forget. I was eight years old. Evening darkness had just descended on our little home in Strongs, a tiny community in Michigan's Upper Peninsula.

My dad called mom, my brother, Don, my sister, Marlene, and me to the kitchen. He then blew out the kerosene lamp we had depended on for so many years. Suddenly, in a room so full of mystique and magic, there was a hush. I can still hear my dad's voice today as he said: "Okay, Jim, you are the oldest child so you get to pull the string for the first time."

I climbed up onto a chair to a spot above the kitchen table where a string hung from the ceiling. I remember a little fear, a butterfly in my stomach. Finally, my courage up, I gave the string a quick jerk.

The room burst into bright light as the bulb at the ceiling shone brightly. The room was brighter than any night before.

I stood there on that chair amazed. There was an intake of breath from everyone in the family. We could not believe it—an event in our lives of miracle proportions.

I am now 65, but I have no more magical memory in my life than that evening in 1940 when our rural electric cooperative, Cloverland Electric, brought electricity to our evening meal for the first time. Mom and dad were so thrilled that they hardly spoke a word throughout that meal. We all kept glancing up to stare at the glowing bulb.

Although I wrote a daily newspaper column for the *Lansing State Journal* for more than 30 years, I have also written a column for this magazine, *Country Lines,* for a dozen years. This magazine goes to all Michigan homes and businesses served by rural electric cooperatives. The very special spirit of rural Michigan and my association with rural electric cooperatives has vastly enriched my life.

That's why I'm pleased to write a forward for a truly wonderful book, *"On Their Own Power."* It is a lively history of Michigan's rural electric cooperatives—the only such history ever recorded to enrich our homes and libraries.

As I write this column today, I am sure that my childhood reflections on those magical days when a new light came shining into rural areas is repeated in the memories of so many others.

"On Their Own Power" is more than a book title. It is a statement of rebirth in rural America. In one way, a 50-year period seems so small—just a short period in history. But in the world of rural electric cooperatives, it has been a long, hard, sometimes very bitter struggle to overcome political obstacles and so many skeptics who said it couldn't be done.

That special spirit of rural electric pioneers prevailed.

It's an exciting story and we found the perfect man to write it. Raymond G. Kuhl has been in the rural electric forefront for 37 years, the last 17 of which he served as general manager of the Michigan Electric Cooperative Association. Ray retired in January 1996, but he still had a mission. He wanted our lives and our libraries enriched with an insightful history—never before written—about the arrival of electricity to rural Michigan and what it has meant to tens of thousands of people.

A list of Ray's accomplishments in this field is several pages long. He was born in Sioux Falls, South Dakota, and was a 1955 journalism graduate of South Dakota State University. He has served in many important roles on state and national levels as manager, writer, and public relations director for the cause of rural electrification. He also helped organize some of the first rural community water systems in South Dakota, an experience he believes was akin to that of the electric cooperative founders.

In March 1997, Ray was honored before 10,000 people at the National Rural Electric Cooperative annual convention in Las Vegas. He was presented the Clyde T. Ellis Award, the highest honor given for outstanding work in rural electrification.

That was a great moment for me and my wife, Darl, because we have grown to treasure the friendship of Ray and his wife, Jackie.

With great confidence, I say you are going to love reading this fascinating story that is researched and written so well.

Co-ops Know How To Lend A Hand

July/August 2001

There have been many prideful moments in my nearly 20 years of association with Michigan's electric co-ops. But the most emotional moment came two days after Christmas last year as my wife, Darl, and I traveled south through Indianapolis, Nashville and Memphis.

We began noticing large convoys of electric utility trucks—10 to 20 of those big rigs in a row—all heading south. Nameplates on their doors said they were from places like Traverse City and Lima, Ohio.

Our curiosity grew and grew until we stopped for the night at a motel in Nashville, Tennessee. There in the parking lot were a dozen of those large trucks. I found one of the drivers and I asked him what it was all about. "We are on our way to Arkansas and Oklahoma," he said. "They are in big trouble in an ice storm that put so many families out of electricity. It's the Christmas season, you know, and we all feel bad for them. We are going to help."

"Yes, but it is the Christmas season for you guys too," I said.

"There is a difference though," he replied, "our families are comfortable and warm back home. Down there in Arkansas and Oklahoma they are buried in four inches of ice—a terrible thing for families."

The next day, we found ourselves passing another big convoy of trucks and I noticed the name on the doors said "Michigan." Frankly, I got a bit emotional. I lowered the window and gave each one of those guys a thumbs up and a honk of our horn as we passed. They made me darned proud.

When we got south of Memphis, it was the same thing in reverse. Now we were meeting convoys coming up from the south. Their nameplates were Alabama, Georgia and the Carolinas. Wow! What a country, I thought. Give this land a crisis of that kind and everyone jumps in to help.

Back home in the spring, I asked Mike Peters, general manager of the Michigan Electric Cooperative Association, about it all.

"Yes, Jim, that's the way we all do it in a crisis. We have mutual aid agreements with our neighbors in and out of our state. You do your neighbor a favor in his time of need and you don't even think about ever needing that favor returned, but we all know there will come a day when we need the same kind of help. The entire country could learn a great lesson from our rural electric cooperatives," he said. Amen to that, Mike.

A couple of quotes come to mind:

"Light is the task when many share the toil." —*Homer*

"Nothing makes us feel so strong as a call for help."
—*George McDonald*

And somebody once said: "When a person is down in the world, an ounce of help is better than a pound of preaching."

Speaking of nice people, Darl and I have admired the character of the Cajun folks in Louisiana. We love to stop in Lafayette and get out to the rural areas where good Cajun music, food and friendship abound. They are all family oriented and anxious to show any stranger a good time.

On our last trip there, we took a swamp tour—out among the alligators, snakes and cypress trees. What a treat. I asked our boat guide what kind of snakes they had there in the swamps. "Two kinds," he said, "big and little." He went on to say the poisonous ones have eyelids for opening and closing and the non-poisonous ones don't have eyelids. "I never know which is which," he said, "because I don't get close enough to tell."

The cypress trees are amazing. We learned that the cypress does not mature until it is 200 years old and there are many of them more than 2000 years old. One tree somewhere in that area is so large that it takes 23 people with arms spread out to get around the tree.

Cajun folks don't fear alligators. They like to eat 'em. I cringed at that until we ordered alligator tail in a restaurant. Delicious. Sort of a cross between chicken and fish.

Alligator hunting season is open only in September. They go into the swamp and hang a dead chicken from a branch just above the water. In the chicken is a hook tied to a rope. The hunter comes by and shoots the hooked alligator and it becomes leather boots, womens' purses and a restaurant delicacy.

The hunters who are good at it make out quite well—about $200 per foot. One guy there caught 56 of them last September. Don't fret, there is not a shortage of alligators. There is a shortage of cypress trees, however, and most southern states have a ban on harvesting them. The cypress has long been in demand by ship and furniture builders because the wood resists disease and insects and it never rots.

Man alive, you can sure learn a lot reading this column.

The Secret Life Of Neebish Island

March 2003

Where in the heck is Neebish Island?

That was my question when I had a call from Warren Geralds, who said the folks at Neebish Island wanted me to be a guest speaker.

"Neebish is Michigan's best kept secret," Geralds said. "The Island is four miles wide and seven miles long. It is in the St. Marys River about 20 miles downriver from Sault Ste. Marie. It has 55 hearty souls who live here all winter and about 300 who live here in summer. You'll love these folks. They are a special breed. They are a throwback in our history. They depend on each other and take care of each other."

So I went to Neebish Island and spoke to the Neebish Island Improvement Association. It was a blast. Everything Warren Geralds said about them was true.

I talked with Cliff Tyner, 74, a lifelong resident who might qualify for one of those "Most Unforgettable Character" articles in *Readers Digest*. Tyner's language turns the air blue, but he is loved and respected. He operated and owned the island ferry for 39 years until that service was taken over about a dozen years ago by the Eastern Upper Peninsula Transportation Authority. That agency also operates ferries to Sugar Island and Drummond Island.

"Island life is tough all year, but it is especially bad in winter. Wimpy trolls from Lower Michigan and other southerly places can't hack it here—too far from shopping centers and Wal-Marts," Cliff said.

Among the 55 winter residents are only two children of Russel Tyner. "They are home-schooled because the ferry has to shut down when the Soo Locks closes on January 15," Tyner said. Courtney, 13, complained to me saying: "Gosh, Mr. Hough, I'm the only 13-year-old on the whole island all year." Her brother, Hunter, is seven.

For the past 12 years, the 12-car ferry has been operated by Bob and Mary Schallip, married 29 years and still arguing over who is boss. She says he is the ship captain and he says she is the ship captain. Together they are the lifeline. They carry a defibrillator and oxygen in their car for emergencies because the boat makes only about seven to nine trips per day.

"But we run her anytime in an emergency," Bob said. "This is not like an eight-hours-a-day job. It is more like a calling. We can't get away much, but we love it and you couldn't get us off here with a winch."

Schallip has served on the Cloverland Electric Cooperative board for the past five years and has high praise for that organization's service to the Island.

Only five persons leave the Island daily to go to work at Sault Ste. Marie. One of them is an island lifelong resident, Les Laitinen, Chippewa County Road Commission superintendent for the past 18 years.

"I don't use the ferry much because I like to be at work real early in the morning. I jump into my boat and shoot across the river where my car is parked on the mainland, I have been doing that for years, even before I went to work at the road commission," he said.

Laitinen says he will always be an island resident. "This is a great place with great people. We have our own fire department and community building and good roads. We have only one church on the island, but it is a dandy and 75 years old this year. Although it is Presbyterian, our Sunday service finds folks of all religions there—Catholics, Methodists, Jews and more. We get along great," he said.

Nancy and Ron Adams have a long island history. Nancy said her family has been on the island for seven generations.

"My mother was here in 1900 and, in those days, the

island's year-round population was about 250. We had four schools. Population and activity here has shrunk over the years," Nancy said.

In its heyday, the Island boasted stores, businesses and resorts as the lumbering era thrived. With the big trees gone, farming took over with only moderate success in such a short growing season. Great fishing, especially for perch, kept the Island a tourist hot spot, but the fishing went to pot years ago and business and tourist life diminished.

Neebish is an Indian word meaning "boiling water." Until 1905, the river had rapids as it passed the island. Construction of the Soo Locks caused a river reconstruction in what has been called the "Rock Cut." The River is now about 30 feet deep to allow travel of the big ore boats.

After the ferry shuts down on January 15, life on the island makes a monstrous change.

"In most years, we can make an ice bridge from the island to the mainland. If the ice gets six inches or more thick, we can cross with snowmobiles and later with cars—sometimes for as long as a month or more of winter," Tyner said.

"We plow the ice bridge and mark it with Christmas trees. We have never had an accident on the ice bridge but it gets pretty spooky in the spring when the water starts over the ice," he said.

Schallip says there may be something to this global warming because the ice has not formed there in recent years. "We have operated the ferry all winter in three of the past five winters—with a vastly reduced schedule, of course. When we have to shut down in January, we give everyone lots of warning so they can stock up with groceries, booze, propane gas and so much more. Then we settle in for a long, quiet and beautiful winter," he said.

Want to buy a ferry boat? Although Tyner has not operated his six-car ferry in recent years, he still cranks it up now and then. "She's in great shape and I'll sell 'er for a mere $65,000. Some people pay that much for a pleasure boat," said the colorful Tyner.

A Family Tradition

November/December 2003

The public service and popularity of Carl Eagle is legendary in Michigan's eastern Upper Peninsula, but his special importance to hundreds of kids in his neighborhood is an untold story.

For kids in a four-mile area, Eagle has been Santa Claus for nearly a half century.

"Actually, this Santa thing has been going on for nearly a century," Eagle says, "because my father, the late Roy Eagle, did it for nearly 50 years. I have just kept it up for the last 40 or so."

His wife, Anne, known hereabouts as Mrs. Claus, bags more than 100 packages of candy and other gifts for the kids, and Carl gets into his Santa suit, hitches up the old horse and sleigh, rings the bells and makes home visits to the delight of the kids. Each child can sit on Santa's knee and visit about their wishes for Christmas.

"It's a blast. I have never had so much fun. Recently I overheard a child's response when some other kids were trying to tell him there was no such thing as Santa. The child said. 'There is too a Santa. He's Mr. Eagle. He comes to my house every year.'"

A visit with Eagle, 71, makes you wonder how he finds time for his Santa role. He has been a Cloverland Electric Cooperative board member for 42 years. He farms 500 acres. He has a thriving farm machinery sales business. He drove school bus for 38 years. He served on the county board of commissioners. He is on the Soil Conservation District board, and so much more. Oh, and don't forge that he served for 15 years as a Justice of the Peace. He is active in the Elks, American Legion, Disabled American Veterans and Lions Club—not the end of the list yet.

How does he find time for Santa?

"Oh, I'd never disappoint the kids. It gets tough some years with the weather and health. One year, a TV crew came out here and the cameraman wanted to ride in the sleigh to get a Santa view of it all. That year, we had a new horse and we didn't know he was afraid of the bells. Santa, the cameraman and the sleigh all wound up in the ditch. It was a close call, but it made a good story," Eagle laughs.

Eagle is proud of his long service to Cloverland, his rural electric co-op.

"I have been on that board for 42 years and I have only had electricity on my farm for 44 years. I remember the days of kerosene lamps very well. Anne and I have been married 42 years and we have enjoyed meeting so many nice people as we attend 25 or 30 meetings a year. Currently, I'm serving as board president. Sometimes, though, I have to be a diplomat and mediate things very carefully. In rural electric cooperatives, every customer is an owner. We have some great employees and they often make me very proud," he says.

Eagle has reduced some of his farming because he suffered a detached retina eight years ago and became blind in his left eye.

"I used to have a feeder cattle herd of about 175 and harvested a monster hay crop. Now I'm down to about 50 head and, at my age, it keeps me plenty busy," he says.

Eagle says he hopes he will never give up Santa.

"The year my horse died was the worst challenge, because that year I also lost my eye and I was attacked and mauled by one of my cows, which thought she had to protect her calf. The animal hurt me pretty bad and I had some injuries that nearly kept me out of my Santa suit. But I made it anyway.

"Anne and I love the kids. The whole neighborhood in a

four-mile area gets involved. They contribute money for the candy and gifts. When it is all over, we have a party to talk it over and plan for the next year. My dad did it 50 years and I'm not far behind him right now. Nothing will put you into the Christmas spirit quicker than the face of a delighted child," he says, with a twinkle in his eye.

Bless The Animals

Loon Lady

July/August 1997

I heard they were calling a retired school teacher the "Loon Ranger" around Munising. So, I went there to find Ruth Warner.

Quickly, I learned that her fascination with loons and her zealous efforts to protect them was not unusual at all. She is part of a growing army of loon rangers in Michigan—all members of the Michigan Loon Preservation Association, a wing of the Audubon Society.

"The loon is the oldest surviving specie of any bird in the world," Ruth said, "and it will take a lot of future awareness to protect them. They abandon their nests when pestered by boaters and curiosity seekers."

Ruth and her husband, Kenneth, live on Little Round Lake near Munising where a pair of loons has annually returned to nest. When she heard their calls of distress as fishermen neared their little lagoon, she became an activist.

She's not a bit shy about giving a gentle lecture to sportsmen and curiosity seekers to explain the fragile nature of loon nesting habits. They produce two eggs and incubate them for six weeks. Any interruption by the public or predators forces them to abandon the nest.

The Association's bumper sticker reads: "The Loon—

Symbol of the North. Preserve it."

Although there was a 60 percent decline in the loon population in the early 1990s, progress is being made. The Department of Natural Resources now has a program to help when a loon ranger reports an incidence of loon disturbance.

DNR biologists go to the scene and place large buoys near the nest to warn the public. The buoys are 61 inches long, 9 inches in diameter and bear the symbol of the loon.

Biologists also help loon rangers build floating nesting islands.

The Association's signs, like the one Ruth put on her lake, reads, in part: "Loon Alert. This lake is the habitat of the Common Loon. Please enjoy wildlife from a distance. If you see a loon flapping its wings wildly and dancing across the water, you are too close.

Consider binocular range as a safe distance for viewing the loon...."

The signs point out that it is a violation of state and federal laws to harass the loons because that action causes one or both of the birds to leave the nest, forcing a loss of the young.

Even my wife, Darl, is a loon ranger. She has a loon call that communicates with the loons swimming in front of our cabin on Lake Superior. She has loon carvings, stuffed loons and pictures all over the place. In fact, her entire kitchen is accented by loons.

They are fascinating birds. They can dive 200 feet and stay under water for up to 15 minutes. They have a wingspread up to five feet long and they can fly 60 to 100 miles per hour. They need a quarter of a mile of water area to get into flight and they cannot go into flight from land. They have two paddling feet growing at the rear of their bodies, making it almost impossible for them to walk on land. Their eyes are red, an important factor for seeing under water. Males are distinguished only by their larger size and thicker neck.

Although their erratic behavior and primitive calls bring

on the expression "Crazy as a loon," their calls are a special language. The wail is a location call. The tremelo and bird laughing call comes when the loon senses danger. The loon yodel is mostly for identification purposes. The hoot, usually done softly, is a communication among family.

The loons live up to 30 years and they winter in the Atlantic Ocean.

For the latest counts of loon population, I called Ed Russell Utych, Executive Director of the Whitefish Point Bird Observatory, an agency of the Audubon Society. Whitefish Point in Lake Superior has become world famous as a counting location for migrating birds.

Utych offered good news. "In the early 1990s, the loon population dropped by about 60 percent, but it has been rising dramatically since 1993, when we counted 3,384 loons migrating between April 15 and May 31. In 1996, we counted 11,728 and about 10,500 in 1997," he said.

The bird observatory staff and volunteers do the counting for the first eight hours after sunrise for the 45-day period each spring and each fall. The above numbers are for the spring count only, but the fall numbers are nearly identical.

Russel says the great dangers to loons are jet skis, speedboats, commercial fishing nets and polluted waters. Autopsies on dead loons often show mercury and lead poisoning. Canada is currently considering a ban on lead hunting shell pellets and lead fishing sinkers.

Meanwhile, the growing army of loon rangers is making a monstrous difference in public awareness. You can join the Michigan Loon Preservation Association by sending $15 to the Association at 409 W. (E) Ave., Kalamazoo, MI 49007.

As the bumper sticker on our car says, the loon is the symbol of the north. Their decline would surely put my household in tears.

Bear Watch

July/August 2000

So, what does a retired Bay City firefighter do in retirement? He starts an 80-acre bear ranch in the Upper Peninsula, of course.

Dean Oswald, 59, now delights thousands of Michigan tourists when he enters the fenced-in area of his land, calls his 14 bears, and hands them marshmallows.

Tyson, one of the bears, weighs in at more than 800 pounds and is considered the largest black bear in the United States.

"I'm like a mom to 10 of my bears because I feed them a bottle and have raised them since they were tiny," Oswald says. "But I don't get near Tyson. He's just too big and unpredictable. Who wants to trust a bear weighing nearly 1,000 pounds?"

After 18 years, Oswald had to leave firefighting because of a disability.

"But that was only the half of it," Oswald says. "I was also a professional boxer and I originated the tough man contest in Michigan. I figured it was time to chuck all that and move to the quiet and peaceful northwoods. I bought this land, which is 9 miles northwest of Newberry in Luce County with beautiful woods and a nice lake. I loved it. Then it happened. I became fascinated by the wild bears. I began feeding them there," he says.

From 1983 to 1997, Oswald fed the wild bears at his home.

"It got ridiculous as so many people came to see them. I figured I might as well make a business of it. I bought my own bears and became licensed by the state and federal governments and opened the Oswald Bear Ranch in 1997. Word has spread and now we entertain thousands of tourists each summer. We charge them $5 per car. I'm not getting rich, but it's a lot of fun and it makes summer jobs for my three grandsons," he says.

The grandsons, Dusty, Zac, and Dean, soon learned there is a lot of expense and hard work operating a bear ranch, and they gave me a lesson in bear habitat. Although the yearlings have to be separated from the adult bears in smaller enclosures, the larger critters roam in an area surrounded by 1,600 feet of high fence. A new, larger enclosure with 233 feet of fence will be open next summer.

"Our biggest problem is not keeping our bears fenced in. The problem is keeping the wild bears from breaking into our enclosures," he laughs.

Several of the bears weigh 500 to 600 pounds, but Tyson, now 11 years old, weighs more than 800 pounds.

"I have owned Tyson since he weighed 3 pounds, but I don't cuddle up to him much. He is just too big to trust," Oswald says as he hands a marshmallow to a ferocious looking 400-pounder.

He says bears can live up to 30 years and the babies are only the size of a mouse when they are born while the mother is in hibernation. The babies cling to the mother. Oswald's bears hibernate from November to March in concrete dens equipped with wood and straw floors. Their diet is meat and vegetables.

"I get very attached to them and they are attached to me," Oswald adds.

Most of the bears just walk behind him, obviously waiting for a treat. "I often carry a fly swatter with me and they respond quickly to a swat from that," he says.

"We actually have a double fence around the bears to keep the public from direct contact. My wife, Jewel, and I carry $1 million worth of insurance in case of an accident with the public, but there is little or no chance of that," he says.

Although most of Oswald's bears are black, the species can produce bears in brown, white, black and combinations thereof.

Like most folks, I am often turned off by caged animal exhibits along tourist routes. The Oswald Bear Ranch didn't seem so bad. My 10-year-old grandson, Colin, was with me on my visit there. I asked Colin what he thought about it. "Well, Grandpa, I think the bears have a lot of free space to run in and they have lots of food and clean water. Besides, they are safe from the hunters who might shoot them in the woods."

What's more, thousands of youngsters like Colin get the thrill of a close-up view of some very big bears.

Oswald laughs at all that. "If we opened the gates, the bears would not leave. Instead, the wild ones out there would be breaking in," he says.

The exhibit is open from Memorial Day weekend through September.

Dog Days

January 2001

It was a beautiful evening in my cabin on the shore of Lake Superior. A crackling fire, a refreshing drink, and quiet time with my thoughts.

Then I looked over at my wife, Darl, and saw big tears running down her face. "What's wrong, honey?" I asked.

"Oh, it's nothing, Jim. It's just that I miss our black Labrador, Candy, so much at moments like this. How she loved to curl up there by the fire, " Darl said.

Suddenly, she had me in tears. Although it's been 10 years since Candy died, we still miss her. That dog enriched our lives for nearly 17 years.

Not long after that experience with Darl, my phone rang. It was my 12-year-old grandson, Danny. In tears, Danny told me their old dog, Sassy, had died. For him, his brother, David, 10, and sister, Ellen, 3, it was the saddest time in their young lives. For my son, Steve, and his wife, Susie, it was devastation. They had Sassy for about 14 years, and she was a great family pet.

I almost recovered from all that when I got another phone call from a person in tears. This time, it was a big, strong, adult, Mike Ennis, a longtime friend of mine who owns an insurance agency in Newberry.

Amid his tears, Mike brought the awful news that his basset hound, Lucy, was killed by a car.

For Mike and his wife Bunnie, Lucy's death was a major tragedy. For so many others—about half the town of Newberry—it was deep sadness. Lucy was such a character that she had gained friends everywhere.

For instance, one of her daily trips was to the front door of the People's Drug Store in downtown Newberry, where she sat and aimed her head high to emit a mournful howl until the druggist came out to give her a dog biscuit. Yeah, Mike, we all loved Lucy.

Because I know there must be thousands of folks out there who also remember a beloved pet, I thought I'd reprint an old poem that often gives me comfort and great memories. The poem, perhaps a half-century old, has an anonymous author, but still says it best. The poem reads:

No muddy footprints on the floor;
Our food contains no hair.
No marks on the windows anymore;
Where a cold nose rested there.
No nest made in a forbidden bed;
No dog to walk in the rain.
No urgent pleading to be fed;
No sweeping hairs in vain.
When doorbell rings no fearsome growls;
No nips at callers' legs.
A fire siren starts no lonely howls;
At mealtimes no one begs.
No barks at rabbits in the woods;
We're free to go away.
A day or week if in the mood;
No Kennel bill to pay.
No sleeping dog by fireplace curled;
When we come in, no fuss.
No eyes to say in all the world;
He loves no one but us.
No wagging tail, no head on knee;
No guard when dankness thickens.
No eager plea for romp or spree;
We miss him like the dickens.

—*Anonymous*

Spring Harbingers

February 2001

After making a speech to an organization in Sault Ste. Marie, I was fielding questions from the audience.

"Mr. Hough, you have written nearly 9,000 columns in your career. Which one do you remember most?"

As I answered that question, I surprised myself—a lot. I didn't think of columns that won big awards and journalism acclaim. Instead, I found myself answering this way:

"It's not just one column. It's a bunch of them over the years on the same subject—first robin sightings of the spring. I came to hate robins."

Well, I suppose the word "hate" is not really in my vocabulary. So let's just say I developed a strong, strong dislike for robins. Actually, it is not the robin's fault. It's that old myth about robins being a harbinger of spring.

I used to wince each time I received calls to my column about the first robin sighting of the year. Those calls started coming in January and they kept up all winter long. Sometimes, I had dozens of "first robin" reports in a day. Each year, along about Ground Hog Day, I'd feel compelled to write another column dispelling that old first robin myth. First robin calls kept coming in anyway.

I wish I had a dollar for every column I wrote quoting Audubon Society bird experts to dispel that old first robin myth. It never worked.

The fact is that large numbers of robins stay up north all winter and flocks of them are often seen in winter way up in Alaska. There are lots of reasons for this, but the biggest factor is home bird feeders. Shucks, any robin with any I.Q.

knows a good food supply when he sees it. Who wants to fly all the way to Florida just to find an earthworm?

So, it all comes down to this: Is the reader calling to report the first robin or the last robin? What I always longed for was the last first robin report.

It was the same for crocus, forsythia, and Easter lily blooms. We got those calls all winter, too—every time the weather got freakish and the south side of the house got warm. Botany folks and florists have long asserted that Easter lilies don't just bloom at Easter. They bloom on the anniversary of the first time they were "forced" in the greenhouse, often not at Easter.

And it still amazes me about the many people who believe all that bunk about the ground hog and his shadow. Others cling to indicators like the hair on the caterpillar or thickness of the fur on squirrels. Bunk, pure bunk. Even meteorologists can't figure out Mother Nature.

There once was a time when the Jim Hough method for predicting spring was flawless. My old method doesn't work so well anymore because my family has grown up and I have lost my enthusiasm for wading into freezing water.

For many years, you could guarantee spring when you saw me tuning up my old Coleman gas lantern and making repairs on my smelt nets.

That's spring, truly spring in Michigan. It was the time when the Hough family gathered at our little cabin on the shore of Lake Superior. We'd climb into heavy socks and waders, pack up hot dogs and buns, toddies for the adults and pop for the kids, and we'd head out to Gallaway Creek.

We'd build a fire and sit around it on a spring evening waiting for that call: "The run is on!"

It was a time of family togetherness and a great chance to wish an ugly winter a fond farewell. Those great moments always came during the last week of April or the first week in May way up north, but a little earlier for smelt fans in

Lower Michigan.

There was a dark side to it all, however: All that back-breaking time spent cleaning buckets of smelt. Whenever we offered fresh smelt to friends, there was always the same old question: "Are they cleaned?"

Sleepless In Paradise

July/August 2002

Because I have had a lifelong fear of snakes, I hereby declare myself the grandfather of the year.

How does that equate?

Because my 13-year-old grandson, Colin, talked me into baby-sitting nine snakes—two-feet to six-feet long—in my home for two nights. Whew! What grandpa ever did a more courageous thing?

It all came about when Colin's friend, Jim McGrath, famed Lansing-area naturalist, was hired to talk on Michigan snakes at the Whitefish Point Bird Observatory near my home at Paradise. Jim invited Colin to go along so he could spend a couple of nights here with his grandma and grandpa.

Near midnight on Friday, Colin rang my doorbell. With sleepy eyes and a dulled brain, I heard Colin say:

"Hi grandpa. We have a problem. They won't let Mr. McGrath take his snakes into the motel and it is too cold to let them stay out in the van. I told him you would let him leave the snakes in your house at night."

Before I knew what was happening, my budding naturalist grandson and McGrath were carrying large containers of huge snakes into one of my bedrooms. Thinking nothing of it at all, Colin readied his bed to sleep in there with the snakes. Good grief, I thought, where is Saint Erho when I need him? Remember St. Erho? The legendary guy who drove all the snakes out of Finland?

I took a peek in there. With widening eyes I saw a big, black rat snake and an albino rat snake—six-footers each—and seven other critters slithering around.

Colin and Jim calmly put some water dishes in there. Jim went back to his motel. Colin was soon snoring in there with his snakes.

Meanwhile, grandpa was lying wide-eyed and completely awake in a bedroom on the other side of the house. I got up to shut my bedroom door. It didn't help. I saw a crack of light at the bottom of the door.

What makes this kid tick? I asked myself. I remembered a recent trip to Lansing in which I slept with Colin in his bunk bed. Next morning, I learned he had a three-foot Corn Snake in there. Its name is "Killer."

My wife, Darl, was much more calm about it all. "Aww, Jim, don't worry about it. None of those snakes are poisonous or dangerous. It's a great thing for a young boy to learn so much from a famed naturalist," she said.

But you haven't heard anything yet. Wait 'til I tell you the rest of the story.

Also with McGrath on the trip were two other teenagers, Glen McGrath and William Gold. Those guys and Colin hung out at my home for much of the weekend. On Saturday, I was sprawled in my lounge chair listening to Ernie Harwell and the Detroit Tigers when I looked up to see each of those boys seated in the living room holding huge snakes that playfully slithered around their necks and into their pockets.

"You want to hold one, grandpa?" Colin asked.

Before I could answer, those boys began a lecture designed to relax me and teach me the importance of Michigan's snakes.

They listed the 17 varieties of snakes in Michigan, including the rat snake, blue racer, water snake, garter, Kirtland, red belly, brown snake, ribbon, Butler, black rat, milk, fox, Green Queen, northern water snake and the Massauga rattler. The latter being the only poisonous snake in Michigan, but with only mild venom.

Colin gave his grandpa an earful with comments like this: "I hate it when people are so paranoid about snakes. All they want to do is grab a shovel and cut off their heads. They should be left alone. They are harmless and very important to our lives as humans."

Next thing I knew, Colin had that monster albino rat snake in my lap. Soon, I was holding it, petting it and getting a kick out of it crawling over my shoulder and around my neck. Hey, this isn't so bad. I think he likes me, I thought. For several hours that weekend, I found myself holding harmless snakes. It was fun.

Later, I had a touch of reality when I recalled my two years in Panama with the U.S. Army Medical Corp. As a sergeant in charge of a medical detachment, it was my job to lecture to the 1,200 men in our regiment on how to recognize the jungle's poisonous snakes and how to treat the bites of such awful creatures as the coral, bushmaster, ferdelance, palm viper, and more. In every one of those hundreds of lectures, I scared myself to death.

But Colin and his buddies taught me a lot in only two days. We plan to repeat the experience next year when McGrath returns. McGrath is a real hero to thousands of Michigan youngsters and adults. After graduating from Michigan State University with a degree in wildlife biology, McGrath began a business at his home in Williamston. He and his wife, Carol, operate "Nature Discovery," a project so successful that he makes hundreds of appearances in Michigan classrooms and even at private birthday parties.

"Carol and I are thrilled because it does more than help us make a living. It gives us a chance to make a difference in future attitudes about Michigan's nature and its living creatures," he said. He has also gained fame with sound recordings of all Michigan frogs. His next project is to record bird sounds so people with visual impairment can enjoy identifying Michigan birds.

"We have already proven that people can identify more than half of the bird species through bird sounds and we think it will enrich the lives of many people with visual impairments," he said.

Cool guy, Jim McGrath.

'Good' Dog

September 2004

An old reporter like me has learned over the years that there is a tremendous reader interest in animal stories. Thus, I can't resist sharing recent letters I received from an old friend.

John Ward was a longtime news editor at the *Lansing State Journal*. He and his wife, Ruth, are now retired and living in Foley, Alabama. For many years, John delighted Michigan readers with columns about life and times with his St. Bernards, Lucy and Mandy. The dogs lived for about eight years and were great fodder for John's popular columns.

John and Ruth were without a dog for many years—until Christmas day last year when their local newspaper told of a St. Bernard puppy, already at 107 pounds, that was found wandering in a ditch. The paper said it would be destroyed if the owner could not be found.

That was too much for John and Ruth. On the day after Christmas, they adopted the dog and named it Bubba. Later, he thought Bulldozer or Houdini might have been better. I thought you might get the same laugh I did in reading John's letters on the "Bubba saga." Following are excerpts:

BUBBA 1. Anyhow, he got his rabies shot and was found to have heart worms and hook worms. He is being treated for these. He weighed in at 107 and the initial vet bill was $107, which figures a buck a pound. If Ruth doesn't quit slipping him extra food and gravies, I'll never be able to afford him.

One night between Christmas and New Year's, we went

out for a quick pizza with our daughter Paula and family. We put Bubba in the screened-in porch where out hot tub is located. When we returned, the screen on the outside door was in shreds. We later learned Bubba had escaped (perhaps Houdini would be a better name), gone down to the neighbors for a short visit, then returned and jumped back through the screen door.

A few nights later, we put him in the garage for the night. The next morning the screen door from the garage to the house was shredded. We got a 20-foot heave chain and tied him to a spruce tree near our garage off the drive. Saturday we went to an observance of the leaving of our National Guard Company for Iraq. We were gone less than two hours. Upon returning, he had gone through our azaleas, Mexican heather and an acuba plant that we had nurtured for six years, as well as a poinsettia. A rototiller couldn't have done a better job.

The vet said he is still a puppy and it may take a year or two more to get him trained. My God, I'll be 75 by then.

Last week, Ruth asked me to call Fr. Keith to come and bless the dog, because she was going to kill him.

BUBBA 2. Bubba has managed to make himself a strong family member. He has been sleeping all night, not like the first two weeks when his crying rousted me from bed anytime between 1 and 4 a.m. to go out and water the azaleas.

On the 14th we took him to his vet, Dr. Dyke, and had him "fixed," as they say down here. He won't be getting any little female dogs in trouble. At the same time, we had his dewclaws removed. These are extra claws that grow from the rear feet, and if not trimmed with regularity, become like ingrown toenails. They grow around in a circle.

Anyhow, he spent a night with other ailing puppies and we brought him home the next noon. He was quite calm, presumably as a result of the anesthetic he received. He was wearing a pair of boots on his rear feet, one blue and the other white.

Meanwhile, we had a man come and fence an area in our

backyard about 30 feet square, using our garden shed as part, which gave Bubba shelter in case of rainy weather (we don't have snow down here). They came on a Saturday and set the posts and poured the concrete and came back Sunday morning and stretched the four-foot high chain-link fence. Ruth and I went to church. Afterwards we had 15 minutes before taking the Eucharist to a dozen ladies in a nearby assisted living center, so we put Bubba in his new, large pen. We then left for the center and gave communion to the group. Before we had reached the final "Amen," Bubba was out heading who knows where. Our next-door neighbor was returning from his church and saw Bubba two blocks away. He stopped and called to him. Bubba came and Charlie walked him home and put him on his 20-foot chain leash in our yard.

In less than 10 minutes Bubba had, with his two front paws, managed to dig a hole under the fence large enough to get his 100-plus pounds through, and took off. Never has a rototiller worked as well as Bubba.

I called a concrete contractor and found that, for $1,300, I could have the pen concreted, or for $700, have a 6-inch footer poured around the fence. I already had $650 invested in the fence. Ruth and I figured the cheapest way to solve the problem was to line the interior perimeter of the pen with 18x18 inch patio stones, which cost $2.97 each at Wal-Mart. They are about two inches thick and weigh about 50 pounds. I made five trips to Wal-Mart for the 60 stones since I was afraid the weight of more than 12 blocks would break the springs on our Lincoln truck.

Bubba seemed to take those in stride. Then, the next day, he had used his nose to push the fence out and was digging outside the blocks. I spent another afternoon wiring the fence to the bottom rail, about every two feet.

With Bubba it is a battle of wits. I think he is winning because we apparently are only half-armed. I told Ruth we would come home some day and find the patio blocks all stacked in a corner of the pen.

BUBBA 3. Many of you, at least one or two, have asked me for an update about Bubba, our St. Bernard. In recent months Bubba has settled down and responded well. In other words, he became a perfect member of our family.

He was smart and I swear could tell time. When I would say, "It's nine o'clock pee time," he'd scoot to the rear door of our home. He greeted our family over the holidays with adoring looks and wagging of his rather strong tail.

Then came 2005. He developed a harsh cough, sort of like the dry heaves. We took him to our vet and when his condition worsened, to another vet on a weekend emergency call. Our vet told us he had a greatly enlarged heart.

Our vet, Dr. Dykes, made arrangements the next morning for us to take Bubba to the emergency room of the College of Veterinary Medicine at Auburn University. We made the four-hour trip and arrived about 2 p.m. Between then and noon the next day, an ICU resident and a fourth-year student ran over 25 tests.

The prognosis is "poor." They sent him home with seven medicines which we try to get him to take, all at least once daily, and some two or three times, to ease his suffering. We were told he might live as long as a year or as short as today, the doctor said he has never known an animal to live more than three years with Bubba's condition.

We plan to make him as comfortable as possible, but when the time comes that his quality of life has gone, we will take the final step.

As Ruth said this morning: "I wish his ornery antics would return. The sparkle in his eyes, etc." And I also agree. After putting our St. Bernard Mandy down a dozen years ago, I said I never wanted another pet that wouldn't outlive me.

I only hope the good Lord has another family in mind to place Bubba. We certainly give Him thanks for sending that lovable dog to us and we also give thanks for the many moments of laughter, happiness and warm feelings Bubba has provided us.

BUBBA 4. Today, April 14, was a sad one at the Ward residence. We took Bubba to his vet, Dr. David Dyke, for what we felt was the best thing we could do for him. We had him put to sleep at 2 p.m. Bubba hadn't eaten in four days nor had he taken any of his medicines. His stomach was distended due to the large amount of liquid around his heart and lungs.

Last night Ruth took him out at 2 a.m. and I at 4 a.m. On both occasions, he stretched out on the lawn, unable to get up and return to the house until he had rested 15 minutes. Where we normally walked twice a day, once for 1 mile and the other for nearly 2 miles. Today he wasn't able to negotiate 50 yards. We remember an admonition once received from our Lansing vet, Dr. F. 0. Grounds: "Don't keep an animal alive for your own sake, but remember his needs."

We figured the best medicine we could give him was to be put down. During the past week Ruth made chicken and noodles, a meat loaf, pizza, Arby sandwiches, roast pork and roast beef for Bubba. These were things he would normally jump at and eat huge helpings. This week he would sniff and walk away without taking so much as one bite.

We didn't stay for the administration of the drug. It would have been more than we could handle. Dr. Dyke is taking care of the cremation for us. He is a fine young man who had also become attached to Bubba and his tears today were also noticed as well as those of his assistant Leigh Ann Ivey, a fourth-year vet student at Auburn who cared for Bubba when we had him to the College of Veterinary Medicine at Auburn in January. Leigh is doing her residency with Dr. Dyke.

Anyhow, in closing, we told Bubba: "Thanks for the wonderful times, the crazy antics and the love you brought to our Alabama home. You will be missed, so very much, but life should now be better for you without pain and suffering."

•

Call Of The Wild

June 2005

Stories like "Little Red Riding Hood" and "Call of the Wild" have no place in the modern debate over Michigan's growing grey wolf population.

That's the position of my neighbor, Cheanne Chellis, owner of three grey wolves.

"The wolf today is colored by all the myths, legends and stereotypes from books by Jack London and such, but the simple fact is that there has never been one documented case of a wolf attacking a human in all of North America," she says.

Cheanne, a native of Harbor Springs, is a paramedic, but her love and fascination for wolves goes back to her childhood. She bought her baby wolves nearly 10 years ago from a woman in Oklahoma whose passion was to save the wolves from extinction. One of Cheanne's wolves was rescued from a fur farm in Minnesota, where wolves were raised for one year before they were slaughtered as fur-bearing animals.

Michigan's growing wolf population is big news these days, with their numbers growing to more than 400 in the Upper Peninsula, and their establishment considered solid in the northern Lower Peninsula (*The Evening News,* Sault Ste. Marie, April 27, 2005). The Michigan Department of Natural Resources says there were no wolves in Michigan during the 1960s, 70s and 80s, but many people claimed wolf sightings here during that period.

Cheanne was grandfathered into a recent Michigan law that regulates private ownership of wild animals, but she prefers to work closely with the DNR and other agencies to ensure safe fences, good veterinary care and good feeding.

In the wild, wolves can live about 8 years, but live up to 15 years in captivity. In order to mate and reproduce in the wild, the wolf has to remain healthy, and that is difficult.

"Most people believe wolves just go around killing things and gorging themselves and that gives rise to the expression, 'eating like a wolf.' But the fact is that only one in 10 of the wolf pack's hunts are successful, and they often go hungry. They eat vegetation and meat, and can eat up to 20 pounds of flesh and then go two weeks without food. They will eat anything from mice to moose," Cheanne explains.

The wolf pack's hunting range can be up to 1,000 square miles, and a healthy wolf can travel 40 miles without rest.

"All dog species originated with the wolf," Cheanne said, "and yet they keep a reputation as dangerous animals. In captivity, they can be dangerous, but not so in their natural, wild habitat."

Cheanne's friend, Len McDougall, has been with the wolves for three years. He loves them dearly, but has been unable to bond with them like Cheanne has since bottle-feeding them years ago.

Len is a successful writer of books on practical outdoor survival, snowshoe use, log cabin building, animal tracking, and more. His eight books are available in stores and online at www.amazon.com. Cheanne also has Alaskan sled dogs.

Len and Cheanne operate Timber Wolf Wilderness Adventures from their Paradise home. They conduct kayak, snowshoe, backpacking, and winter survival classes. They also teach sled dog use and winter camping, and lead day hikes in to the wilderness. Most activities are done by appointment and for a per-person fee.

"Our wolf enclosure is not a commercial venture, although many visitors and Paradise residents make cash and meat donations to help us feed the animals. The Paradise community's acceptance of the wolves is unanimous and heartwarming to Len and me," she says.

My wife, Darl, and I live only a quarter-mile from the wolves and we love to hear their very loud and mournful, harmonious howls in the evening.

The wolf is special. They mate for life. After a male dies, the female will never mate again. Each pack can have large numbers, but there is always a leading male and a leading female. They all work together to feed and protect a new batch of pups.

Despite some claims from cattle farmers and hunters, wolf attacks on livestock are not that common and many such kills are done by packs of wild dogs, badgers, and coyotes, and blamed on the wolves. When a farmer can prove wolf attacks on his livestock, the DNR makes a reimbursement to the farmer and, in some cases, the wolf-gone-bad is hunted down and killed.

Our Whippoorwill

July/August 2005

The night call of the whippoorwill brings out big-time nostalgia for my family. That sound has been special to us for nearly a half-century.

It all goes back to about 1960 when we bought property on the shore of Lake Superior, north of Paradise. Although the property was cheap, we were poor and we camped there on vacations with a tent, pitcher pump, and an outhouse. Those were the greatest days of all, and the nights around the campfire made an unforgettable family bond for Darl, me, and our kids, Linda and Steve.

In those days, our nearest neighbor was more than a mile away. After a full day of fishing, swimming and more, the kids would get pretty sleepy around the campfire, but not a night passed without one of them saying, "Daddy, call the whippoorwill."

I had developed a pretty good whistle imitation of the bird. Soon, we'd hear the return call. As a little time passed, it came closer and closer. Soon, the whippoorwill would land on the roof support of our tent. For long hours, it would serenade us with that oh-so-special sound of "whippoorwill" constantly repeated.

That sound, along with the crackling of the campfire and our family silence, punctuated the ending of another great day up north.

Soon, however, the kids were nodding off and we carried them to their sleeping bags in the tent. During that commotion, the whippoorwill would leave. But soon after the lantern was turned off, the bird returned to sit there atop our tent and make long repetitions of his special call. One night, I burst into laughter when I heard Steve's sleepy little voice come out of the sleeping bag with a measure of disgust. "Daddy, can you tell him to go home to bed?"

The whippoorwill is seldom seen in the daytime. It nests on the ground, amid fallen leaves in an almost perfect camouflage. It is a 10-inch bird that is brown with a black throat. The male has broad-tipped white tail feathers, visible only in flight. The female tail is all brown. The female lays two white eggs with grey and brown markings. They nest in a wide area of the United States, but they winter in Florida and the Gulf of Mexico. At night, the bird's eyes reflect a ruby red glaze in a car headlight. It feeds on night moths and other insects.

However, this special bird that adopted our family became a challenge for us when it nested only 50 feet from our campsite. Mamma whippoorwill sat on her two eggs and did not mind us taking a peek at her now and then. The problem was our beloved Beagle, Scoopy. He did not share our human instincts to protect the bird. What beagle would not have dived into that nest with hunting tendencies in full bloom? So, we had to tie Scoopy up at night, and keep him on a tight leash during the day. Despite his howls, the bird stayed and, one day, we got to watch as the baby birds hatched. That privilege will always remain in the hearts of the Hough family.

Not long afterward, mankind's encroachments ended the sound of the whippoorwill on our shoreline, now dotted with homes and cabins.

For some years, however, we made an annual camping trip to a little wilderness lake in Chippewa County, where the kids could still swim with the loons and thrill at the campfire when daddy successfully called the whippoorwill closer.

Linda and Steve are now in their mid-40s and it had been many years since we heard the whippoorwill call. But a great thing happened to Darl and me last spring. We made a trip to that little wilderness lake one evening. We had a picnic supper and built a campfire. I looked across that fire to see tears on Darl's face. "What's wrong?" I asked. "Oh, I don't know, Jim. I was just thinking of this campsite when the kids asked you to call in the whippoorwill. How about it, dad, can you call the whippoorwill for me?"

After I got my emotions under control, I tried my whistle. It was a bit rusty, but I soon had it going. As darkness arrived, we heard the answering call from three locations around us.

There was no more control. We both burst into tears. Only one thing could have improved on that night—the presence of Linda and Steve.

Please, Lord, protect the whippoorwill.

Life In The U.P.

Don't Knock Da U.P.

January/February 1996

Country Lines editors tell me their readership surveys show that Michigan's lower peninsula residents like to read about the Upper Peninsula. Sometimes I'm not so sure about that.

For instance, I received a letter, unsigned, that said: "All we ever read in your column is disgusting stuff about the Upper Peninsula."

Enclosed with that letter was a long list of anti-Upper Peninsula observations. So, in the interest of fair journalism, I thought I'd better tell a little on the other side of the story. Here are a few of a U.P. hater's views:

- The U.P., I came, I thawed and I transferred.
- If you love the U.P., raise your right ski.
- The U.P., where visitors turn blue with envy.
- Save a yooper, kill a mosquito.
- The U.P., one day it's warm, the rest of the year it's cold.
- The U.P., home of blond hair and blue eyes.
- The U.P., mosquito supplier for the free world.
- The U.P., land of many cultures, mostly throat.
- The U.P., where the unique meet to sleep.
- The U.P., closed for glacier repair.
- The U.P., glove it or leave it.

- The U.P., where you have to jump start your kids.
- The U.P., where you can grow three things–older, fatter and colder.
- The U.P., it's there to protect Ontario from Wisconsin.
- The U.P., home of 10,000 Makis.

There was more but that's all I can take right now.

Sometimes I think folks in the Upper Peninsula fall right into the trap of its critics by making a display of U.P. negatives. For instance, I always thought it was a bad advertisement they put there along Highway 41 between Houghton-Hancock and Copper Harbor. It is a monstrous billboard in the shape of a temperature gauge, a giant graph showing that 309.4 inches of snow fell at that location in the winter of 1978-79. It brags that that equals 32-1/2 feet of snow.

Some yooper ought to take his chain saw to that thing.

* * * * *

Because heavy snowfalls come fast and frequent on the shore of Lake Superior, I often find myself visiting with my neighbor, John Thompson, as our snowblowers meet in the road. For years, I have been amazed at the old and drab knitted hat he wears in winter. One day last winter, I couldn't resist anymore.

"Good grief, John, where'd you get that ugly old hat?" I asked.

Obviously hurt, John explained it this way: "I know this old hat won't win any style shows, but I'll never part with it. It is a treasure. I was issued this hat when I went into the U.S. Navy 53 years ago," he said.

So, don't you think we ought to have an oldest hat contest?

Outhouse Stories

March/April 1996

I broke out in uncontrolled laughter one day recently as I cleaned out an old file cabinet in my little office on the shore of Lake Superior. I came across a yellowed, old folder labeled "Outhouse Contest."

That old file goes back at least 30 years to a time when I was earning my pay in the *Lansing State Journal* newsroom as a daily columnist. I had just bought a piece of property north of Paradise on the shore of Lake Superior. Our family used the property as a camping spot but we needed an outhouse. I got a brilliant idea: Why not use all that amazing brain power in the newsroom to create an exciting design for an outhouse? I put a note on the office bulletin board offering a free beer at the corner saloon for the winning entry in my outhouse design contest.

It must have been a slow day in the newsroom because I had about 20 contest entries. Some were awesome and complex. Others were simple. Still others were too crude to mention here.

That was in the days of our space program infancy, so many of the designs included outhouses that efficiently shot effluent into orbit, incorporating special heat shields to resist burned posteriors on the outhouse users.

Some included glass bottoms for sewage viewing, special racks for Sears catalogs and *Playboy* magazines. One design (an entry by a disgruntled reporter) had three levels: publishers at the top, editors below that and reporters at the bottom of the pit. Another had a large board that slid through the building with various hole sizes for various sizes of posteriors.

The designs included stereo systems, movie screens, warning lights, automatic wipers, telescoping footrests, waiting rooms, splash pits, fur-lined seats, Venus flytraps, reading lights, and fans.

Perhaps best—and too lengthy to include here—were all the pages of verbiage on how to finance the construction and all the special qualifications of the contractors and design companies. All of it written by reporters who had become experts in governmental and educational gobbledygook.

But my "Judges Committee for More Relaxed Bowel Movements" awarded top prize to John Green, whose entry was a shovel with a roll of toilet paper on the handle. John won a beer at the Peerless Saloon and "One Free Pass To The New OutHoughs."

When that newsroom exercise ended, our publisher put his own note on the bulletin board. It said: "If you guys put that much imagination into the production of this newspaper, we'd win a Pulitzer Prize. Get to work."

That summer we built a little outhouse at our campsite. It was simple enough—a little lean-to with a half-moon vent and fly screen. It served us well for many years until a new cabin and modern plumbing came along. But I couldn't bear to burn down the old outhouse. It was an eyesore, I guess, but it still stored my axes and shovels. One day, my wife, Darl, said: "That's it, the outhouse has to go. It looks terrible."

I was preparing to burn it down when a neighbor, Fred Vanantwerp, a retired cop, came along. "Don't burn that, Jim, I want it," he said. What the heck, I gave it to him. We loaded it onto a trailer, and Fred left with it. Next day, I saw my old outhouse sitting proudly on the beautiful lawn of a cottage owned by Guy Avery of Traverse City. When Guy came in for the weekend, I got all the blame for putting that old outhouse in his front yard.

But the tale of my old outhouse has not ended. Avery's neighbor, George Clary, said he wanted the old building to put back in the woods to store some of his hand tools. George, now in his 80s, can still claim my outhouse stands proudly, but in need of paint, there on his property.

"Someday, I'm gonna auction it off when you get famous after you die," George laughs.

I still go look at the old outhouse now and then. So many great memories.

* * * * *

There's the time I brought a carload of state police buddies to my cabin for a weekend of fun. On the highway trip north, they got into a discussion of how cottage owners hide their cottage keys. Each of them had investigated so many cottage burglaries in their careers that they had come to know all the common places keys are hidden.

"I'll bet I can find any hidden cottage key in 10 minutes," one trooper said. "It will be under the door mat, lying on the trim above the door, under the fuel oil barrel, behind the electric meter or in the crotch of a nearby tree," he said with confidence.

I bet him a case of beer he could not find my hidden key if he worked at it all day. The bet was on. He finally gave up his search the next day and I took him to my outhouse where I reached under the seat to take my cabin key off a nail where it was hanging.

"I proved something I have always known, there has never been a cop smarter than a reporter," I said.

"No, Jim, you just proved that reporters like to dig into certain foul materials more than clean cops do," he said.

But I won the case of beer. I didn't share it either.

One retired state trooper friend, Art Tooley, had an exceedingly popular outhouse at his cabin just south of mine on Lake Superior. Art ran electrical wiring to his outhouse, where he kept an old refrigerator filled with Strohs beer. It was handy there. Trouble is, Art's outhouse got too popular and he had to put a padlock on it. That didn't help, though, because any smart, old reporter can find a cop's hidden key.

Great outhouse stories abound in most families. My mother always told of the time my brother, Don, took his new and tiny puppy into the outhouse with him. The little dog fell down the hole and mom had to fish it out with the hoe. She said the puppy's ensuing bath was one of her hardest child-rearing moments.

Dad liked to tell of the time he decided to build a new outhouse. When the new structure was finished, he set fire to the old one. Soon afterward he was in shock to see his four kids out there roasting hot dogs over the fire.

My Welcome Sign Is Out

May/June 1996

"A good journalist can write a whole lot about any subject."

When I was recently inducted to the Central Michigan University Journalism Hall of Fame, I ran into an old journalism professor who made that quote in one of my classes over 40 years ago. But I never believed it. Nobody can just sit down and write a lot about any given subject.

So I thought I'd sit at the typewriter today and put it to the test. Let's see how much I can write about a toilet seat.

However, I won't write about just any old toilet seat. I'll write about a very special toilet seat that has hung on a tree at the entrance of my driveway at Paradise for about 45 years.

Way back then, I was a daily columnist for the *Lansing State Journal* and stuck with problems of privacy brought on by the high profile and community celebrity status of a daily byline in a big paper.

Our family treasured our short vacations here on the shore of Lake Superior, and we found it hard to share so much of it with readers who couldn't resist stopping by to visit and check out our digs. And yet, we did not want to hide from close friends.

So, we took an old, black toilet seat that was headed for the dump, painted red stripes on it and hung it on that tree. There, we said, that's our sign. Tell friends to look for the toilet seat.

It worked perfectly and Paradise business people regularly told tourists they had no idea where we lived.

About 15 years ago, my longtime friend, Whispering Bill Anderson of the Grand Ole Opry, visited me at Paradise and asked about the toilet seat. After I explained it all, Bill's face took on a stern look and he said, "Jim, my friend, you will never in your life get a bigger compliment than when a fan asks you for an autograph. I know you want privacy, but it is a sin to hide from the folks who made you successful."

When Bill left, I painted my name in big, white letters on my black mailbox and put another "Hough" sign on the front of my garage. What's more, I never regretted it. My buddy Bill would stand out all night in the rain to greet his fans if that was what they wanted. His lesson stuck with me and I have found it fun to visit with strangers who show up in my driveway to request an autograph on one of my books.

One day in midsummer, an old man came to my house with a book he wanted signed. I was in bed ill at the time, but my wife, Darl, could not send the old man away empty. She asked me to come out to meet the old man and sign his book.

He said to me: "I want you to sign right here on this page in your book—the page that has the great column you wrote about your dad." I did his bidding and then asked his name. Suddenly, I realized I was talking with one of my father's best friends. They were competing milkmen in Lansing, so many years ago, and they had a cup of coffee together at a restaurant every morning.

Needless to say, I kept him in my home all day. Thanks, Bill Anderson, that old toilet seat would have failed me that day.

But the old toilet seat still hangs there proudly as a sign for some and as a special reminder to me that one must never forget any of the rungs that are climbed to success.

And so, *Country Lines* readers all, you are super special to me. If you are in the neighborhood, please stop in.

I have a special association with another toilet seat—one hanging on the wall in the workshop of a dear friend, Jim Decker. Jim used his old toilet seat as a frame for a large picture of me. He hooked a string to the toilet seat lid. When the lid is tied up, Jim is happy with me. When he has not heard from me for months, he drops the lid.

The lid is up right now. I just called to check.

Duel With Superior

November/December 1996

Although 21 years have passed since the Edmund Fitzgerald went down in Lake Superior, there is still an untold story about that terrible storm. It is a story of fear, near-death, horror and heroism.

Our true story involves six Native Americans who were tending their commercial fishing nets on that fateful day, about 20 miles from where the Fitzgerald and its crew were lost. That day in Whitefish Bay, Nov. 10, 1975, began pleasant enough, but let's let our hero tell his own story.

The man is John Lufkins, 53, administrator for the Bay Mills Indian Tribe at Brimley. He doesn't like to talk about it much because the horror of it all still remains. As a favor to me, John granted an interview at his office, and told the story this way:

"I was 32 years old then and doing some commercial fishing with Pat Kinney, who was a young man of 18. The day began as a typical November morning, crisp and clear. The Lake was relatively calm, a good day to launch the boat and tend our nets out in Whitefish Bay near Tahquamenon Island, a tiny piece of land a few miles northwest of Brimley.

"We got out there and began lifting a net when, all of a sudden, the lake began to boil and churn enormously. It was like nothing I'd seen before. I told Pat to drop the net without even resetting it. We quickly headed to the island where we knew there were a couple of old abandoned shacks. Our plan was to wait it out. Well, we waited and waited and waited. We played cribbage and made coffee in the shack but the storm only worsened.

"Suddenly, we were amazed to have the shack door open and in walked Billy Cameron, soaked and nearly frozen to death. We were shocked. We didn't know anyone else was out there fishing. Billy told us his boat had capsized in the storm and that his fishing partner, Andrew LeBlanc, was still out there.

"We ran to the shore. Sure enough, there was Andrew floating toward shore and hanging on to a gasoline can. We quickly grabbed him and got him inside. Both men stripped down and warmed up.

"I asked Andrew and Billy if there were any other fishermen out there. They said 'no' and I believed the others had made it safely back to the shore west of Brimley. But, just to be sure, I decided to take another walk around the island. The waves were so high by now that you couldn't see much. I got back to the shack and, just as I started inside, a monstrous blast of wind tore the tarpaper off the shack. I grabbed the door and hung on. I feared the shack would be blown away. As I tried to shut the door, I looked out and saw someone out there. We had no idea who it was.

"Billy and Andrew were exhausted. Pat and I knew it would be pure suicide to go back out there in the 16-foot boat.

"I told Pat to stay because he was young with a lot of life ahead of him, and I don't know yet today what made me do it. My body was in it, but my mind was kind of numb. I got a life jacket and got into the boat. I started to the area where I thought I had seen the person. A short distance out I realized I was about to sink in that small boat and that I had forgotten to put the drain plug in. I returned to shore, put in the plug and started out again. By now, I had no idea where to find anyone in that awful, boiling sea. I was blown around several times, losing total control of the boat. It was simple enough at those moments–I knew I would die. There was no chance.

"Suddenly, there in front of me were two men frantically hanging onto a capsized boat. They were my uncle, Francis

Parish, and his son, Christopher. At that time, Francis was near 50 and Chris was in his early 20s.

"By then, they had been in the water two or three hours. They were nearly unconscious. They had little strength or awareness. I yelled to them that I would bring the boat between them and that one should grab each side so as not to capsize my boat. But when I got there they were too exhausted to do anything. So I told them to hang on and I'd try another approach. I came at the boat from the other side, revved the engine and ran forward in my boat. I grabbed Chris and, somehow, I threw him into the boat. He collapsed there and I ran back to the motor. By then, the boat with my uncle had again disappeared.

"Soon, however, I found the boat again and ran up to it and asked Chris to pull his dad aboard. But he had no strength left. So I made the same move as before and ran to the front of the boat. Somehow—I'll never know how—I grabbed him with my left hand and pulled him aboard. He was like a rag doll and just fell into the bottom of the boat, his legs in the air.

"I got the motor started and tried to figure a direction to the island. In that black, awful sea, I could see nothing. Chris asked me if we were going to die. I tried to comfort him by saying I hadn't come out there with plans to die, but the real truth is that I thought we were goners. The waves were 20 feet high, and finding the island was like finding a needle in a haystack.

"Suddenly, there it was. I headed for the lee side of the island and was nearly there when a wave threw the boat into a rock and sheared a pin in our motor. But we were close enough for Pat to throw us a line and we made it in. All I remember about that moment was the feeling as my feet hit that shore. My knees began to shake and my body wobbled and I collapsed right there.

"We cooked some fish to survive. We figured somebody would come after us. Nobody came. We tried to sleep. We thought we heard a helicopter in the night and ran out but we had no way to signal. Next morning, about 7 a.m., we figured we'd try to make it back to the mainland. We had a little radio with an almost-dead battery. We caught a newscast about the Fitzgerald sinking with 29 men aboard and we knew nobody was looking for us. We were all reluctant to get back into that 16-foot boat, but we thought we had a good chance to make it. About halfway in, bigger boats came out looking for us and we all made it home later that morning," he said.

Paradise Welcomes Snowmobiliers

January/February 1997

Five feet of snow fell in three days at Sault Ste. Marie in early December. It made national news. They brought in the Michigan National Guard. It was a calamity.

Meanwhile, 70 miles west of the Soo, an equal amount of snow fell at Paradise and Whitefish Point. But it was no big deal. Folks there just pushed the white stuff aside and prayed for more. Heavy snow there is a Godsend that puts grins on the faces of business people that you couldn't wipe off with a snowplow.

Fact is, few winters pass without 20 feet of snow at Paradise. One winter, it went over the 27-foot mark. And so it is routine—and a matter of economic survival—to know you can always find snow at Paradise when it is scarce elsewhere in the state.

All that makes Paradise the state's snowmobile Mecca. If you'd like a motel room or cabin on a weekend in Paradise between Christmas and the end of March, you'd be smart to get a reservation a couple of years in advance.

"Snowmobiling accounts for 60 percent of the motel, restaurant and gas station business here each year," says Chris Kruizenga, owner of Heidi's Travelers Motel.

Susie Frettner, owner of the Shell station and convenience store, says she is always amazed to look out her store window at nearly 100 snowmobiles lined up at the gasoline pumps. "They come here from Ohio, Indiana, Pennsylvania and other places, but mostly they come from southern Michigan. It is not uncommon for 3,000 snowmobiles to pass through our town on a weekend," she says.

Tom McBryde, a Chippewa County deputy sheriff assigned to Whitefish Township, has to "walk a tight line" between vigorous enforcement and tolerance. "In recent years I see a whole lot of good, clean, family winter fun going on here. Our township has about 150 miles of groomed trails that join up to a network of 6,000 miles of groomed trails in the Upper Peninsula. It is nothing for some of these folks to ride 200 to 300 miles a day. They can go anywhere from the Soo to Copper Harbor and they do it routinely," McBryde says.

The busiest time in Paradise comes during the Christmas and New Year's holidays, when most motels and restaurants are filled with family groups.

"Although we have to arrest about 80 riders a year for off-trail encroachment on private property and highways, we do our best to recognize the majority who are enjoying good, clean, safe fun," McBryde says.

Whitefish Township has recorded one snowmobile accident death in the past 12 years. "I can say with confidence that 85 percent of our accidents are caused by young riders speeding and the other 15 percent are caused by inexperienced riders who don't know how to handle the modern, powerful sleds," McBryde says.

In past years, snowmobilers had a reputation of going from tavern to tavern and sipping peppermint Schnapps in between. All that has changed now. The same drunk driving laws that apply to motorists now also apply to snowmobilers.

An aged log tavern, the Yukon Inn, is a Paradise landmark and a popular stop for snowmobilers. Its owner, Tom Archambeau, offers this perspective: "It was always a small percentage of customers who had bad behavior because they drank too much. Now, with the new laws, that percentage of bad guys has shrunk and there is a larger measure of responsibility. In all, our business has not diminished. They come here for more than a drink. They know we have the best hamburger in the north. At one time last winter we counted 184 snowmobiles parked in our lot."

Wilderness trails in the township take snowmobilers to the Tahquamenon Falls winter splendor, to Lake Superior's ice, and into wooded areas inaccessible in summer.

In many ways, the snowmobile tourist has saved Paradise. Not many years ago, you could shoot a cannon down the town's main drag and hit nothing in the winter. Now the local grocery store owned by Mike and Joanne Cook remains open all winter with enough business to pay the heating bill. A similar spin-off hits Tracy Augenstein's hardware store and other businesses.

"It all helps our summer business, too," Kruizenga says, "because those winter visitors come back to see what the place looks like in summer."

Township residents have provided a high-powered sled for McBryde to catch violators, and the township ambulance service has an "extraction sled" equipped to carry injured persons out of remote areas.

On the hood of Tom's big sled is a picture of a coyote. Below that it says: "Beep Beep, you're busted."

Snowmobiling is high-tech and high-cost these day. Thus, the folks who do it are folks who can afford it.

"They are welcomed because they are good tippers, and for the most part, awfully nice people," Kruizenga says. "The average snowmobile costs more than $6,000, and the accessories of radio-equipped helmets, suits, boots and mittens cost more than $600. Most parties arrive in town with four to six machines on a trailer. Add gas, motels and food into all that and you can see it's expensive," he says.

But I have talked to hundreds of them and it is really not complicated. Snowmobiling is their passion—just like boating, golfing and skiing is to others. They hit town and can't wait to unload those sleds and head to winter splendor.

But my wife, Darl, and I prefer the quiet crunch of our snowshoes in a snow-laden woods. Some backaches and winter cold limit us a bit these days, but we still put high priority on a snowshoe walk on a moonlight night.

Da Scoop On Dose Yoopers

January/February 1998

They call themselves the "Dorkmeisters of Musical Merriment," and they certainly are the most unusual folks I've met in my long writing career. They are "Da Yoopers"—the Upper Peninsula group that's both outrageous and delightful.

Da Yoopers bombed onto the American scene direct from their Ishpeming digs to be featured on more than 2,500 radio stations and concert halls nationwide. Who hasn't heard "Second Week of Deer Camp," or marvelled at "Rusty Chevrolet," and "Smelting U.S.A."

Traveling along Highway 41 at Ishpeming, you can't miss the monster sign that says: "Da Yoopers Tourist Trap. Free Toilets." Other signs tell you that Jim DeClaire is "Da Head Guy," who invites you to stop and dump your cash at the Tourist Trap.

Below that big sign is Gus, world's largest chain saw. The place is loaded with equal nonsense, but it drags in tourists equal to the flow at Taquamenon Falls.

I asked a tourist from Pennsylvania why he stopped."I love these guys," he said. "They poke fun at themselves and they are among the most talented and creative musical groups I know."

Jim DeClaire, 52, known locally as "Hoolie," heads the group and is the big idea man.

"We have a mailing list of about 45,000 now, and a distribution network for our music, books, shirts, and other stuff," Jim said as he stood near a sign for tourists that says "please don't move up here."

His number one musical colleague and longtime business partner is Lynn Coffey, owner of a degree in public relations.

"We toured the country with our wacky band for nine years," Lynn said, "and the business grew beyond us. We realized a year ago that we had to take a couple of years off the road to settle down and create some videos and other studio innovations. We will probably go back on tour again, but it's a hard, stressful kind of life."

Other Yooper members are Lynn's husband, Jerry Coffey, along with Jim Bellmore, Danny Collins, Bill Langson, Dick Bunce and Don Dishno.

When I interviewed them, they were deep into videos for "Second Week of Deer Camp," "Rusty Chevrolet," "Smelting U.S.A.," and more.

"One very major effort for us right now is our Christmas album," DeClaire said. "It will be pretty outrageous with some novel lyrics. We feel we have a great shot at getting a holiday hit out of it. There will also be a serious Christmas song or two," he said.

The Christmas album has a song about the latest toy fad—"Rinky Linky Dinky Doo Dad" and a "Super Dooper Yooper." Another tells how "Grandpa and Grandma Got Run Over by a Beer Truck." Another new album features the "21st Century Yoopers in Space."

I'm handicapped trying to portray their Yooper accents and special Upper Peninsula language featured in the songs. "We don't make fun of Finns, Swedes, the French or any group. Our Yooper language, spoken by everyone hereabouts, is a mixture of all those things. We'd never put anyone down. If we ever laugh at any group we are laughing at ourselves," DeClaire said.

Coffey said there is sometimes a local resentment or misunderstanding. A local Chamber of Commerce official objected to their sign proclaiming a "tourist trap," but "we told them to go get a sense of humor."

DeClaire said he thinks "it's amazing that you have to go way off to another state to find people who understand what we are trying to do. Folks back home are often the last to discover you."

A sense of humor for sure, but they admit it's a bit more goofy than others. An old snow blower sits at the entrance to the Tourist Trap. A sign says, "You'll never hear a Yooper say it is safe to put the snow blower away." A direction board on the wall lists the distances of towns and cities all over the country. It says Hurley, Wisconsin, is "3 cases of road pop and two brush stops west." It says New Orleans is 2,299 miles south. "Watch out for crabs. We have such crawly things in the U.P., and you don't want 'em in your shorts."

They even produced a book, "You Know You Are a Yooper When. . .," with lines such as: "You know you are a Yooper when you can ski out your upstairs window."

They list the Tourist Trap as "one of three wonders of Yooperland." They can't remember the other two.

Outrageous or not, the Yoopers and their wares have wide appeal. *The New York Times* has printed an article about them, and they are featured in many advertisements. Currently, they are getting monstrous exposure in Strohs beer ads, each with wonderful humor.

How serious are these guys? Here's how they describes themselves in their brochure: "Da Yoopers, the dorkmeisters of musical merriment, are unique and original entertainment at its insufficient." The "Emil Aho Dictionary" defines Da Yoopers as "the ultimate garage band. They are independent stupid dorks who do their music in any style they choose and play to an audience from ages 8 to 80, with 2,500 radio stations playing their stuff. And they *still* practice and record in the garage."

Once A Troll, Always A Troll

May/June 1998

It's amazing how many trolls are trying to be Yoopers these days. A "troll" is a person living below the Mackinac bridge. A "Yooper" is a native of the Upper Peninsula.

There are a few trolls who claim they have become Yoopers, but it takes a long, long time and a ton of verbal restraint to become a Yooper if you ain't been born and raised here.With the decline of mining and lumbering, there was a 50-year period during which the U.P. lost population with every census. But a big change has come in the past 20 years with a vertical population explosion. Mostly, it's folks retiring from the grind of the Lower Peninsula and moving north to Yooper serenity.

But the trolls moving north soon discover they are foreigners. They don't understand the natives—their language, their severe winters, their general suspicion of trolls.

A typical troll does everything wrong because he brings his Lower Peninsula behavior and attitudes north with him.

He is thrilled to purchase a piece of land on Lake Superior or a lesser lake. But he quickly puts up a "no trespassing" sign and a chain at the driveway. That irritates the Yooper.

It's not the troll's fault, of course, and I suspect that this kind of cultural and living clash is occurring all over the United States as hitherto undeveloped areas struggle with what so many call "progress."

The troll somehow feels his mission in life is teaching these backward Yooper hillbillies how they ought to change their lives.

He tells how he moved here to enjoy the clean air and

beautiful night skies over the lake. Then he installs a giant outdoor mercury light that turns the beautiful night sky to an artificial brilliance. His giant mercury light doesn't just light his yard. It lights the yards of a couple of neighbors on each side.

"Why'd ya do dat?" the Yooper asks.

"Because of security. Bright lights at night keep burglars away," the troll answers.

"Burglars? Burglars? Here, where nobody locks their homes or cars? Here, where we had only one breaking and entering in the township in 17 years and the deputy caught that guy before he got to M-28? Why ya gotta come up here and screw up the country? I'm gonna shoot out that light," the Yooper yells.

Yep, they come here and fill the land with "no hunting" and "no fishing" and "no trespassing" signs. Heck, some even destroy the natural beauty of a lakeshore by installing a mowed lawn. Man alive, if any lawn resembling those in Lower Peninsula subdivisions show up at my yard, I'm gonna get a bucket of Agent Orange and kill it quickly.

And so it goes and so it will continue. It's a clash of cultures. Everyone means well. But the Yoopers still get great pleasure when a troll sells out and moves back to Flint after a summer battle with mosquitos, black flies and a winter battle with snow and cold.

In fairness, there are thousands of trolls who become Yoopers by making a quiet and gentle move into a community. In just a matter of a few years, they are accepted and looked upon as Yoopers. But most trolls find conflict quickly.

And it's amazing how soon some claim to be an authority on the U.P.

Recently, a troll who moved to my community only a couple of decades ago criticized one of my columns by saying: "You folks who move from down below shouldn't be so quick to comment on how we natives like to live up here."

That got me. Imagine a troll with only 20 years experience suddenly becoming an expert Yooper. I couldn't resist. I gave him a little lesson on how you become a Yooper.

I told him how my grandfather, Dan Hough, was traveling along Eckerman on a train in the late 1800s when he met my grandmother, Eliza Brissette, daughter of Francis Brissette, who was stationmaster and postmaster at Eckerman for 17 years. Grandpa and grandma moved to Ozark and Trout Lake where grandpa was a farmer in summer and a logger in winter. My dad, the late James Hough Sr., was born there at Ozark as the seventh child in the family. He met Myrle Schultz, daughter of Herman Schultz, foreman of the railroad crew at Trout Lake. They were married in Engadine and I was born at Trout Lake in 1932 in a house a little north of the present Catholic Church there. Dad and Mom moved to Raco, Soo Junction, Newberry and Strongs. Dad was a longtime Chippewa Township clerk and was employed as a railroad and highway worker. Aww, that's enough. With all that Yooper heritage, no troll had better be calling me a troll.

There are a lot of trolls I like. Some are even very close friends. But I never let them forget that they are still trolls.

More About Yoopers & Trolls

November/December 1998

There was an amazing reaction to a column I wrote several months ago, headlined "Once a Troll, Always a Troll."

In the column, I poked a little fun at the "trolls" who move from the lower peninsula to Yooperland and bring along their city ways—no trespassing signs, mercury vapor yard lights, lawns and demands that the Yoopers change their lives. Although there were some serious sides to the column, it was mostly a humorous look at what Yoopers perceive as a cultural clash.

Both sides took the column far more seriously than I intended it. Some trolls (those who live below the bridge) were furious with me. We had a lot of mail and phone calls. But, in the end, response was about 10 to one in support of the Yooper position: "Don't move up here and bring your city ways to screw up our land."

I'm a little embarrassed because the column has been widely reprinted in the U.P. publications and church bulletins. "John Voelker would be proud of you," said one Yooper.

The late Voelker, an Ishpeming native and former member of the Michigan Supreme Court, is better known as Robert Traver, author of "Anatomy of a Murder" and other great U.P. stuff. He often lamented "those flatlanders who come up here and ruin our trout fishing." Voelker gained fame through the monthly meetings of his "Let's Blow Up The Bridge Committee." His gang never got to bridge destruction but they drank a lot of brandy and played a lot of cribbage.

That's the spirit in which I chastise the trolls. Come on, you guys, where's your sense of humor?

My wife, Darl, and my son and daughter also objected. "You have been married to this flatlander from Charlotte, Michigan, for 44 years and I think I know more about the U.P. than you do," Darl said.

"Harrumpf," I said.

What's more, my grandkids want a "grandkids' exclusion from trollism." They were all born "down below," but they think of themselves as Yoopers. Well, there are born-again Christians, so maybe we can have a new category—born-again Yoopers.

* * * * *

Anyway, I'm going to ramble on to another Yooper-related topic.

Religious intolerance rears its ugly head often. That's why I can't resist a few remarks about the way they do it in Paradise.

In March 1994, a little Catholic Church called Our Lady of Victory suffered a serious fire. As firemen battled the blaze, Rev. Donald Bates, pastor of the Methodist Church nearby, arrived on the scene to find a group of Catholics in tears. He comforted them and offered his church for their services until repairs were made. The Catholics gratefully accepted and held services at the Methodist Church for many months.

But that's only part of the ecumenical lesson Paradise offers. Before and since the fire, the area Lutherans borrowed the Catholic Church for their services. Imagine that. In the old days, Martin Luther and the Pope were not exactly on speaking terms. "We get along great. We need each other so much these days," said Lillian Weaver, a longtime, staunch Lutheran. For nearly 20 years she played the organ at the Catholic Church services. "It always felt good to me," she said.

Several years ago, a Paradise Methodist Church pastor was married to a Catholic woman. He accompanied her to Saturday Catholic services and she attended his Sunday Methodist services. No problem.

When Our Lady of Victory Catholic Church celebrated its 50th anniversary recently, there was a great ceremony with several high-ranking Catholic leaders present. But they also included Methodist Pastor Bates. In that ceremony, Pastor Bates led a prayer for the future of the little Catholic Church. It was a touching moment and a great lesson for all.

On every Good Friday and every Thanksgiving Day the Catholics, Lutherans and Methodists of Paradise join in an ecumenical prayer meeting. The ceremony rotates annually from church to church. Enough said. The religious world can take a lesson from another kind of Paradise.

I like a quote from Frederick the Great: "All religions must be tolerated for every man must find his way to heaven in his own way."

Meanwhile, Pastor Bates has retired in Iowa and the little, old Catholic Church is soon to be torn down to make way for a new structure in Paradise. When it's dedicated, I'm betting the Catholics will invite Methodist Pastor Bates back, along with leaders of other local churches.

Michigan's Best-Kept Secret

March/April 1999

Shhhh! Don't tell anyone, but I'm about to spill one of Michigan's best kept secrets. I just can't resist because it is enough to pop the buttons of every prideful Michigander.

You've probably never heard of Robbins, Inc., in Ishpeming. It's a little hardwood flooring mill in operation since 1947.

Now, get this. Here's the shocker. That little factory has made basketball courts used today by 21 National Basketball Association teams and has made nearly 80 percent of all the basketball floors at America's major universities.

What's more, it made 200,000 square feet of portable floors used at the Atlanta Olympics and it also made floors for the 1988 Olympics in Korea, and the 1992 Olympics in Spain.

All that, not to mention all the athletic floors in high schools, YMCA centers, church recreation centers, roller rinks, ballet, aerobics and fitness centers in this country, and in many others.

Bill Latva, plant manager and a 32-year employee, was bursting with pride as he showed me through his plant.

"We have 115 employees and a high percentage of them have been here more than 20 years. It is the best and most prideful work force in Michigan. We make between five and six basketball courts here per day—all on one shift. Yes, Jim, the whole state of Michigan should be proud of what we do here," Latva said.

A main ingredient, of course, is the high quality of the

maple forests in the Upper Peninsula and Canada.

Robbins' company pride begins at corporate headquarters in Cincinnati, Ohio, with the president, James Stoehr.

"Our Ishpeming plant ships the flooring to Cincinnati where it is assembled into portable floors.

"When the Chicago Bulls moved from Chicago Stadium to the United Center, we tore up our old floor and installed a new one at the United Center. That's when Michael Jordan took much of the old floor, including the center jump circle, and had it installed in his home. Heck, even the boxing star Evander Holifield has our flooring in his home," Stoehr said.

The average Robbins All Star Portable basketball floor costs about $100,000.

"There is more to it than maple boards," Stoehr said. "Today's floors are very high tech. They have several inches of underlayment that includes rubber cushions. We do enormous research to determine the impact of a 240-pound man landing on our boards. Research shows that players can practice twice as long and prolong their careers when they play on a cushioned floor that they can land on after a high jump in the air," he said.

Robbins has a flooring institute in Cincinnati where prospective customers—from dancers to athletes from several sports—can choose a floor to their liking.

The Ishpeming work force figures it has produced nearly 30,000 basketball courts in the past 20 years.

"I went to the NCAA tournament last year at Lexington, Kentucky," Latva said, "and I admit it kind of got me to watch them play on a floor we had produced. Fact is, more than 80 percent of all NCAA Division I tournament games last year were played on Robbins' floors," he said.

When I talked to Jay Cooper, Robbins' public relations man, he made this claim: "Our floors are at the foundation of every basketball championship in America."

There's no argument. Robbins put the floor in the new

Michigan State University Breslin Center and MSU won a Big Ten title. Least surprised about that was MSU head basketball coach Tom Izzo, because he is a native of Iron Mountain—just down the road from Ishpeming. As a Yooper, Tom would give credit to his U.P. flooring.

Another amazing thing about the Ishpeming plant is that it collects all the wood dust and scraps to burn as fuel to heat the plant in winter, and to create steam needed for kiln drying of the boards. The leftover steam is then used to power large, old generators to create electrical power for the plant. In off-hours, the electrical power generated is sold to the U.P. Power Company.

Good grief! I never should have told that story here because that puts Latva and his crew in competition with those of us in the electrical co-op field. Awww, what the heck, I admire that little plant anyway. One thing is for sure, it's a reason for Michigan pride. What say we ask for our Michigan Week organization to honor Ishpeming for "Michigan Product of the Year."

It's 20 years overdue.

Proud Work If You Can Get It

March/April 1999

Just like the cowboy, the lumberjack has passed from the scene—almost overnight.

That reality struck home with me recently as I visited with Dean Conklin, 50, of Eckerman, a tiny community in Chippewa County.

"I haven't worked since September and my unemployment has run out. The job my father did all his life and the job I have done since I was 16 has now gone from the American scene," Conklin said when we visited in December.

The lumberjack has been replaced by a big machine called "The Processor." It motors up to a tree, cuts it off at the ground, trims the limbs and stacks the sticks of pulpwood.

"It's quite a story when you think about it," says Conklin. "It began with the strong belief in a guy called Paul Bunyan and his blue ox, Babe. Now it all ends in machinery that does four times the work of one man in the woods."

In the late 1800s and early 1900s, pine was king in Michigan, and so many other states in the U.S. There were many small railroad spurs hauling huge logs out of the woods and off to a world market.

But the real strength was the two men with their axes and crosscut saws who bravely felled the trees. As major logging came to an end in forest depletion, the pulpwood cutter took over.

"We had lots of names over the years, but we called ourselves piece cutters or stick men. We were paid by the cord or by the stick of pulpwood, an 8-foot-long log prepared to go to a paper mill somewhere. Everything in our lives was measured by those terms. When one of my kids broke a toy, you could hear my wife, Ila, lecture them by asking 'do you know how many sticks your daddy had to cut to buy that toy?' It was hard work but it also kept food on the table and a truck in the yard for thousands of us," Conklin said.

Conklin recalls that his first lumberjack job came at age 16.

"In those days, we used our axes and a buck saw or bow saw. Later the chainsaw. With a good chainsaw, some of us could cut from 10 to 15 cords a day and make over $200 a week. Now the modern machinery marches into the woods and produces 40 cords a day," he said.

Until very recent years, men like Conklin lived in lumber camps owned by the lumber companies. They were given food, shelter and payment per cord.

"Our family often had to live in the woods in some pretty rough homes. I missed the 5th grade in school because our family had to stay in the woods. Eventually though, I graduated from high school. I have had a good life in the woods—beautiful nights, wonderful quiet scenery and a strong feeling of independence. Now, I have to admit, I'm scared. What can a 50-year-old guy like me do now?" he asked.

Laughter filled the room as his wife, Ila, chipped in: "He didn't tell you about being out there when it was 40 below zero and snow 10 feet deep. He didn't tell you about the blackflies, mosquitoes, yellow jacket nests, deer flies, horse flies and the constant risk of terrible injury from falling trees and sharp blades."

But they agreed that it was a good life—but without hospitalization insurance or retirement benefits.

"I am proud of one thing though. I worked for myself and I worked for a number of timber companies for many years, but I only applied for and received unemployment benefits three times, each for short periods. Being on a dole wrecks a man's pride. I wanted no part of that," he said.

Few lumberjacks were lazy. As Conklin put it, "You never got paid for sitting around."

Timber harvesting was then, and still is, today, a year-around job.

"In deep snow, we had to shovel out around the tree trunk before cutting because we were not allowed to leave a stump. Yeah, winters were hard, hard work, but I liked having a job," he said.

Conklin worries about his future because he fears he has few skills to offer an employer. This old columnist doesn't see it that way. Conklin had to become an expert mechanic and so much more as an independent businessman in the woods. He even had to become a great cook. "We had to learn to make a meal out of nothing lots of times," he said.

But none of that counts as much as his willingness to work. I'm hoping that some employer figures that out soon and offers a job to Dean Conklin and so many other rugged Americans who find the lumberjack fading into history.

I like an old quote from Ulysses S. Grant: "Labor disgraces no man, but occasionally man disgraces labor."

But a quote from Joseph Conrad probably says more about a man like Dean Conklin. Conrad said: "A man is a worker. If he is not that, he is nothing."

Troll Talk II

March 2001

Yeah, yeah, I know how the trolls hate it when I expound on the virtues of the Upper Peninsula. But I just can't resist.

No matter where you travel, you can't escape the Yooper influence. My wife, Darl, and I were in the Rio Grande Valley of Texas last winter when we heard there was to be a gathering of Yoopers at Alamo, Texas. So we rounded up a few other Yoopers in our trailer park and headed to Alamo. Nearly 300 Yoopers were there.

"If somebody dies in the U.P., they'll have to send down here to get pall bearers," said a Calumet man. All of the 15 counties in the U.P. were represented. Heck, we all knew each other—almost. What a great afternoon—a chance to share a refresher course in Yooper language and eat a pasty.

Meanwhile, similar Yooper gatherings were being held in Houston and such places as Gulf Shores, Alabama; Fort Myers, Florida; and Green Bay, Wisconsin. Wherever Yoopers roam, they will always find each other.

The movement got so strong in Mobile, Alabama, that Gene Owens, a popular columnist for the *Mobile Register* newspaper, suggested that Mobile needed "A U.P. sister city." Response to this was overwhelming, and the Alabama folks chose Escanaba. It began by sharing newspaper stories in the *Escanaba Press* and the *Mobile Register,* but the ties have become stronger each year. What fun for all!

Notice, if you will, that there are no Lower Peninsula clubs in those places. No, sir. Only Yoopers seek out each other and share that kind of loyalty to their homeland.

Perhaps the most famous Yooper gathering has been in Lansing, where the Upper Peninsula Club of Lansing claimed memberships exceeding 1,000 people. It began in the 1950s—in the days when Yooper teams often won state high school basketball championships. The Yooper club held a big lumberjack pancake breakfast at the Lansing Civic Center to honor those teams each year.

When the U.P. club died because of a shortage of leadership in the 1980s, I used my *Lansing State Journal* newspaper column to revive it. Our first meeting was attended by about 80 people. The next month, attendance went to nearly 300. For many years after that, the annual pasty dinner drew crowds up to 1,500.

You can take the kid out of the U.P., but you can't take the U.P. out of the kid. No, sir. Like it or not, trolls, that's the way it is.

At our Yooper banquet in the Rio Grande Valley—more than 2,000 miles from the Big Mac Bridge—they passed around the tale of the "Yooper Creation Story." It goes like this:

"In da beginning dere was nuttin'.

Den on da first day, God created da Upper Peninsula.

On da second day, He created da partridge, da deer, da bear, da fish and da ducks.

On da third, He said, 'Let dere be Yoopers to roam da Upper Peninsula.'

On da fourth day, He created da udder world down below.

On da fifth day, He said, 'Let dere be trolls to live in da world below.'

On da sixth day, He created da bridge so da trolls would have a way to get to heaven.

God saw it was good and on da seventh day, He went huntin'."

* * * * *

Because the history of copper mines in Michigan's Upper Peninsula has fascinated me in recent years, I found myself visiting old mines and mining towns.

Historians claim there was a time—in the late 1800s and early 1900s—when Calumet, in the Keweenaw Peninsula, was larger than Detroit.

It is still fascinating to visit the long-abandoned Quincy Mine at Hancock. The mine, now a tourist park, was once the deepest mine shaft in the world, plunging more than 9,000 feet down.

We took our grandkids there a couple of times for a guided trip deep underground. Tour guides demonstrate the awesome dangers and hard work experienced by miners in those days. Some of what they endured is hard to believe. I recommend a visit to the Quincy Mine. You and your family will jabber about it for weeks afterward.

Most of us who grew up in the U.P. are somehow linked with those old copper and iron ore mines. Several relatives on my mother's side were long-time miners.

Darl and I have some long-time friends, Bill and Carol Perry of Marquette. Recently, Bill and I were talking about the old days of mining. He told of his father, Bill, working all his life in mines around Ishpeming and Champion. I told Bill that is the area where my uncle, Sterling Schultz, worked in the mines. Bill was astounded. After he got his breath back, he said: 'My God, Jim, do you know that my father and your uncle were a two-man mining team for many years?'

Wow! Another small world story. Uncle Sterling and Bill's dad are both dead now, and no wonder. Long life was not a product of careers in the mines.

Snow In Paradise Is Not For Winter Wimps

January 2002

One day last February, I received a phone call at my winter digs in the Texas Rio Grande Valley. "Hey, Jim, this is Ben Musielak, your neighbor in Paradise. I just thought I ought to tell you this is a record bad winter up here in the Upper Peninsula. Right now, a snowdrift completely covers the travel trailer in your backyard and my dogs just walked up a snowdrift and over the roof of your house," Ben said.

I couldn't resist. I had to give my friend a bit of Yooper winter perspective.

"Come on now, Ben, 200 inches of snow there is no big deal," I said. "Trouble is that folks like you have been spoiled in recent years by mild winters in Paradise. Some of us, a little older than you, gained achy muscles and wore out snowblowers there with up to 326 inches of winter snow. Heck, Ben, that's 27 feet of snow in one year in the early 1970s, seven feet more snow than you have there right now," I said.

My outburst brought silence from Ben. I hated to burst his bubble, but 200 inches of snow in the Upper Peninsula is a long, long way from any record. The Keweenaw Peninsula holds the record with nearly 400 inches in one year. As a kid growing up in the eastern end of the U.P., I remember winters when the highway was just a ditch with snowbanks 10 feet high on both sides. My mom always told of the time she had to cancel my birthday party on March 30 because there was a 30-inch snowfall and blizzard.

There were many times during the past 40 years that we came to our cabin on the shore of Lake Superior only to discover that the cabin could not be seen. On one occasion, I recall shoveling for two hours before I could get the cabin door open. Once inside, there was nothing outside any window except a complete wall of snow.

Yes, I'd say winters have been quite mild for many years up here in Paradise.

I was cleaning out an old file in my office recently when I found a column I wrote for the *Lansing State Journal* in April 1985. I thought I'd reprint it here because it tells of a 20-inch snowfall here on an Easter weekend. I dedicate it to all you modern-day winter wimps. It read, in part:

Rotten. Absolutely rotten.

That's the answer I gave to those who asked me about my vacation on the first day back.

We left here March 28 on a beautiful spring day. We arrived in Paradise to find two feet of snow and a broken water pipe in the cabin. The refrigerator wouldn't work. We had a trailerload of doors, windows and other materials for an addition we're putting on the cabin this summer. We hauled all that heavy stuff from the road to the garage, sinking deep into snowdrifts with each step.

Sunday arrived—my birthday. My present was a 10-inch snowfall and howling winds. Couldn't find the car the next day. Everything was buried in snowdrifts. The sun came out. It melted enough to allow us to drive out of there. We went to Sault Ste. Marie to buy a refrigerator. Hauling the new one in and the old one out over all that snow was an endurance run.

About midway in that project, a question suddenly occurred to me: Who needs a refrigerator in that country anyway?

Weather forecasts are less than accurate in the U.P. On Good Friday, the radio said we might get three inches of snow on Saturday. What actually came was the worst blizzard of the entire winter at Paradise.

The winds howled all night and another 10 inches of snow

fell. I couldn't push the cabin door open in the morning. I put on the snowshoes and made a trip to find the car parked out on the road. What car? Where? Everything was buried. I found the car by poking around with the end of a snowshoe.

I went back into the cabin and called the Chippewa County Road Commission. "You guys gonna get a plow in here today or Sunday?" I asked.

"You kidding, mister? We won't get a plow in there before Tuesday. We have two of them broken down and we can't even plow the main road. This is the worst blizzard we've had. You'll just have to stay put," the man said.

Good grief. What if I couldn't get back to work on Monday? What if the folks up in Clinton County heard that the Onlooker had a "snow day" at Paradise?

I made a toddy, threw another log on the fire and turned on the TV set. The Tigers-Reds exhibition game was on. It was the first inning and Milt Wilcox had walked the bases full with two out. Suddenly, the electricity went out. The wind had blown a tree over the power lines.

I made a frantic call to a friend in Paradise, five miles south of my cabin. "I've got to get out of here," I said.

So, a rescue unit was formed. Raymond Monk, Robert Woodrich, Denny Bedell and Wayne Shooltz made a train of four-wheel drive trucks and pounded their way down my cabin road. We packed up the dog, the cat, the groceries and a few clothes. We locked up the cabin and faced the biting wind and snow. Those guys hooked onto my car and trailer and hauled us out.

We got to Paradise and stayed the night at Wayne's home. Sunday dawned bright and clear and the plow had been through the main road. We headed home.

I heard they had spring tornadoes down in Lansing country. Spring is a long way off at Paradise. Winter is still raging there.

Paradise school was closed last week, too, but only because it was the regular spring vacation.

Launch A Laugh

May 2002

Looking for a real good belly laugh? Just spend an hour or so at a busy boat launch area. You'll be in stitches in no time.

My favorite "launch laugh" location is the city marina at Sault Ste. Marie.

Recently, my wife, Darl, and I sat there for an hour and had to leave because our sides hurt from laughing.

Here are a few examples. One guy backed his boat trailer into the water while his big black Labrador dog, Fred, was riding in the back of the truck. Fred, fearing he might be left on shore, jumped out of the truck and into the boat. The motion caused the boat to leave the trailer and float out from the dock. The owner, seeing his plight, jumped out of the truck, tripped and fell into the water. He got up sputtering and yelling obscenities at the dog. "Fred, you get that boat back here right now." But, of course, Fred couldn't start the motor and another boater had to rescue Fred and the boat. Once on shore, Fred got a tongue lashing you could hear all the way to the Chippewa County courthouse.

Typical cases, of course, are those in which a prospective pleasant evening boat ride by a couple turns into a whopper argument. "Ethel, you blankety-blank dummy, back the car down here properly." "Carl, you idiot, once again you forgot the beer..." "What? You left the fishing worms back home in the garage?" "It's a darn good thing you can't start the motor, Clyde, because you left our son back on shore."

We watched a big family dog leap out of a boat to hit the water with a big splash and begin swimming in pursuit of a mallard duck. Dad blamed mom. Mom blamed dad and the kids screamed their fear, but they finally got old Fido back into the boat.

Of course, no boater, including me, can deny similar experiences in their own life. There is just something about boat launching, I guess. I recall the time many years ago when my son, Steve, was about 12. We launched our boat at the mouth of the Tahquamenon River. Steve was in the boat while I drove the car and trailer up to the parking area. As I returned to the boat, Steve was standing up and screaming, "Dad, you didn't put in the drain plug. I'm going down with the ship." Talk about a quick trip back with the trailer. Whew!

The episode most talked about at Paradise occurred about 20 years ago when a local bar owner, Don Compeau, launched his boat at the Tahquamenon River for some evening fishing. He backed his car and boat trailer down to the launch site and set his car brake while he got out to release the boat. That's when the car brake failed and the whole thing—car, trailer and boat—rolled into the river where there was about 12 feet of water. Don, known locally as quite a character, had a good audience as he jumped on the hood of the now floating car, leapt over the car roof and landed inside the boat. He quickly started the outboard motor and attempted to drive the boat, trailer and car back to shore. But it failed and down went the car. They say the car headlights could be seen shining for a long time down there at the river bottom. Later, a wrecker pulled the car out. They say Don got it started again. Nobody recalls whether or not he got the brakes fixed.

But you won't find any boat launching foolishness at the public harbor near Whitefish Point on Lake Superior. That's where you find the real pros—scuba divers from all over the country who come to the shipwreck coast—Lake Superior's graveyard.

Lake Superior waters off Whitefish Point have become a scuba diver's mecca. I have often visited with amateur and professional divers at that boat launch and found their stories fascinating.

While the Great Lakes have claimed over 6,000 shipwrecks, a 15-mile area around Whitefish Point offers more "diveable" wrecks than anywhere in the world, although Micronesia's Truk Lagoon has about 40 Japanese warships that were sunk in World War II.

Although the "Edmund Fitzgerald" is the most famous shipwreck in the Whitefish Point area, it is far too deep for normal scuba divers. Most of the wrecks they dive on are steamers that collided in fog or had boiler explosions and went down in the late 1880s.

Today, modern electronic directional equipment, weather forecasts and radar make shipwrecks rare. The biggest factor, of course, is radar.

The Price Of Paradise

September 2002

The splendors and wonders of life in Paradise and Michigan's Upper Peninsula have long been extolled in this column under my byline. Maybe it is time I gave you a little of the other side of that story. How about the period from Memorial Day to July Fourth—a time of horror and pure hell.

By the end of July, those giant, ferocious mosquitoes and black flies are a dim memory to most Yoopers, but not this guy.

I hate 'em with a special passion. I have long threatened to take a vacation to some other part of the world in the month of June.

During that period, there is a long row of spray cans sitting on my back porch. The labels say Raid, Off, Deep Woods Off, Cutters, Muscol, and more. My June bill for all that stuff is probably $50.

And don't forget my headnet. I have to put that thing on just to get to my roadside mailbox. Black flies seem to last only a couple of weeks, but those mosquitos—man, how they chew on me; each bite leaving a welt the size of a quarter.

Last June, two bad things happened. First, my doctor said I needed to treat my back troubles with a daily morning walk of two miles. Second, June of 2002 brought the worst crop of mosquitos in Yooper history. Oldtimers in their 90s say they've never seen them this bad.

But, my back was hurting and I wanted to follow my doctor's advice. Each morning I took a bath in mosquito dope, pulled on my headnet and headed out for a walk on my backroad. I don't think the bombed trenches of Vietnam,

Korea and Europe could have been much worse. Torture, pure torture. But I never missed a day. It took real guts and there were not many of those left when the mosquitos got done with me.

It helped my back some, but I don't think I have the resolve to do that again in June of 2003—good back, bad back, or whatever. I'm not leaving the safety of my screened-in porch.

My grandkids bought a special t-shirt for me. It has a giant mosquito on the front and a label saying "Paradise Air Force." On the back of the shirt are hundreds of mosquitoes and a big, red, bloody spot labeled, "Gotcha."

Yes, I have managed to find and describe the beauty of Yooper blizzards and otherwise hated things in this land, but I hearby confess that June up here brings little but pure horror.

My Chamber of Commerce friends and those who depend on tourism won't like this, but I have been inducted into the Michigan Journalism Hall of Fame as an honest reporter, so I have to tell it like it is. Sorry.

And, here's how it is: If you are a parent of small children and you head up to the U.P. on a camping trip in June,

you need more than mosquito dope. You need a psychiatrist. You are pure whacko. Your kids won't go outside your tent and you'll soon be heading home with the kids in tears. And don't bring them to my screened-in porch. I'm out of room.

Now that June 2002 is over, I am going to ignore all those warnings about the stock market and failures of so many giant corporations. Instead, I'm doing some research into products like Off and Cutters. Those guys must be getting rich. That's where I'll invest—skeeter dope and headnets.

The t-shirt business is also good here. In addition to the one I described earlier, there are some other good sellers. Another shows a big red cross and a mosquito. The label says: "I gave blood in Paradise, Michigan." Still another shows a big mosquito with a label saying: "Suck it up. You are in the U.P."

Yoopers have long been amused by downstate tourists who come here dressed in shorts and t-shirts. Long sleeves, long pants, high boots and the stench of skeeter dope are the dress code of the Yooper. Whenever we see a tourist wearing shorts and standing there, talking with you amid frequent pauses to slap their legs, we call it the "tourist dance."

I am amazed, though, at how much little kids tolerate those bugs. My six-year-old granddaughter, Ellen, was with us for a week in the thick of the mosquitoes, but she played outside every day. She loves to call in the seagulls and feed them table scraps. I watched her down there at the lakeshore calling the gulls and ignoring the cloud of mosquitoes around her head. Grandpa couldn't have taken that for a minute.

A neighbor of mine, Jack Purcell, describes it this way: "We slap mosquitoes all summer so we can stay in shape to shovel snow all winter."

If that's true, the spring of 2002 has us in great shape for a terrible winter.

Rainbow Lodge Thrives Beyond The Lines

January 2003

They say you should never bite the hand that feeds you, and I fear I may get into hot water with this column. It might not go over well with my bosses at the electric cooperatives, publishers of this magazine.

But I can't resist telling you about my visit with Richard and Kathy Robinson, who say their rural electric cooperative refuses to provide service to them.

"We're just kidding, Jim, the fact is that we live 15 miles from the nearest rural electric line and it would cost our co-op nearly $300,000 to bring us service," Richard says.

The Robinsons have displayed a real pioneer spirit for nearly 40 years in operating the Rainbow Lodge at the mouth of the Two Hearted River on Lake Superior, 32 miles north of Newberry. Their nearest neighbor is six miles away.

"Many of the tourists stop here to say they are lost. Then they ask how we can stand to live out in the middle of nowhere. That always makes me a little mad because we are quite comfortable and we are actually living out in the middle of somewhere," Kathy says.

Since it's not economically feasible for Cloverland Electric Cooperative to bring electricity to the Rainbow Lodge, the Robinsons make their own power with huge generators, solar panels and a windmill. Propane provides heat and lights.

"Our success here is due to the primitive nature of it all. Folks love to come here to get away from phones and television. Families love the great fishing, canoeing, rock hunting, hiking, and a chance to see a moose, bear, deer and more,"

Richard explains.

Snowmobilers find the Rainbow Lodge a perfect place: motel rooms and cabins with cooking facilities, plenty of wilderness trails, a gas station, fully stocked store and a café.

"While our customers love the idea of roughing it here, we are not as primitive as it might seem to an outsider," Kathy adds. "The fact is we have a telephone line, and a satellite dish at our home for all the television advantages of our friends in the city. We have refrigerators and deep freezers. We could put TV sets in the cabins and motels but our customers don't want them."

The Robinsons have also raised a family in this location. Beth, 16, is still at home and a student at Newberry High School, more than 30 miles away.

"Our road is plowed all winter by the Luce County Road Commission and they do a great job. There are some days, however, when the plows can't get through amid storms and heavy drifting. We get along just fine in a storm. We have no power outages, so long as we keep a good supply of diesel fuel for our generators," Richard says.

The school district will even send a bus to pick up Beth daily, but the Robinsons say that Beth prefers to spend many nights in Newberry with her grandmother to avoid missing after-school activities.

"Now Beth is old enough to have her own car and she hates the dreaded bus," he says.

The Robinsons may be self-sufficient in the wilderness, but it did not come without a price. "These things cost us a lot—$12,000 for solar panels, $6,000 for eight industrial batteries, big bucks for two large generators, and all the propane gas and diesel fuel. Our generators use about one-and-a-half gallons of fuel per hour and we run them about eight hours on a normal day," Richard says.

The Lodge property covers 40 acres surrounded by state land, and has an airstrip that gets about a dozen landings per year. Also included is a campground for tents, trailers and motor homes—$10 per night with water and a "state of the art outhouse." The outhouse walls are adorned with beautiful wilderness paintings done by a local artist. The women's side features eagles and the men's has loons.

The Robinsons say business is good, with over 15 percent of their patrons returning after their first visit.

"The Two-Hearted River is truly special and more than an Ernest Hemingway legend," Richard says. "In spring and fall there are the great steelheads for anglers and many like to fish from the Lake Superior shore for salmon and menominees. In summer, fishermen love the Two-Hearted and its many feeder streams for trout," he adds.

Kathy says the most common comment she gets is: "My God, I haven't slept that good in months." Lake Superior air will do that to you.

Kathy says another frequent worry of city folks is: "Good grief, what would our kids do without television and computers?" Kathy says that almost without exception the children find they don't have time for TV because of new adventures in the outdoors and a new relationship with their parents in the evenings with games and conversation.

The Robinsons don't live a reclusive life. Both are emergency medical technicians and they have a first responder ambulance in the garage that's used to perform an important community service. Kathy also serves on the Newberry School Board and Richard serves on the Newberry Tourist Council.

Sorry, all you electric co-op folks. You may not be as important as you think. The Robinsons are doing just fine without you.

"Careful, Jim, don't overdo it," Richard says, "We'd still like to have electrical service out here."

Family & Friends

Learning A Lot Of Things

September/October 1995

Here's a thought: Labor Day weekends don't depress me anymore.

Wow! Zowie! Shazam! Labor Day weekends always depressed me in the past. That weekend usually found my family at our cottage on the shore of Lake Superior at Paradise. As the weekend ended, we all realized summer was over. Time to head back to the city grind: roar of loud motorcycles, sirens, squalling brakes, back to the work grind, back to school and plenty of worry about repairing the billfold after all the vacation expenses. Not to mention the immediate financial crunch of buying back-to-school clothes for the kids. Woe was us.

I remember one return to my newspaper office after Labor Day weekend. I was griping and moaning when one of my cynical colleagues observed that our money worries had only begun. "There are only 109 shopping days until Christmas," he said. But, alas, all those ugly memories are dim and distant. Ah, the wonders of retirement on the great shore of Lake Superior. All those tourists are gone home to worry about back-to-school clothes. They left just when the fishing is getting good and the splendid fall beauty in the Upper Peninsula is upon us. Ah, life is good. Sorry about that, all you working stiffs.

Retirement is great fun—if you can stay busy. As someone once said: The worst of work nowadays is what happens to people when they cease to work. And another anonymous quote says: The best time to think about retirement is before the boss does.

I figure a man is known by the company that keeps him on after retirement age.

Don't let a gloating retiree depress you working stiffs who head home from vacation. Instead, do what all of us did for so many years, and give thanks for a good summer of family fun. I am deeply grateful for so many summer vacations. One Labor Day weekend still stands out as very special in my memory. It came 20 years ago when my son, Steve, was 16. Earlier in the spring, he had asked permission to live at our Paradise cabin all summer and work in a restaurant where he had been offered a job as a dishwasher.

We debated the idea and worried about it a lot. Finally, we decided such an experience might be good for him. In any case, it beat his lying around our Lansing house all summer.

So, Labor Day weekend arrived and we went to our cabin. I had not seen Steve in several weeks. He had changed. He proudly told of the $500 he saved and I noticed a much stronger handshake as he greeted me and said: "Dad, I want to thank you and Mom for letting me stay at the cabin this summer. I learned a lot of things."

"Such as?" I asked.

"Well, I learned what it means to work hard and that it is not easy to earn money. But most of all, Dad, I learned that I miss my family," he said shyly.

Yes, sir, there have been some great Labor Day weekends in my life. That might have been the best.

* * * * *

After a recent visit with my neighbor, Brent Biehl, I realized how fickle success can be. Sometimes it hinges less on the quality of your product or your talent than it does on something as fragile as a label.

Brent has been on a 17-year battle to market a "hardwood loggette" made of sawdust to compete with charcoal. His story might make a clinic for entrepreneurs who struggle for public acceptance.

As I pondered Brent's long and expensive struggle, I thought about a singer some years ago. What was his name? Eugene Dorcey, I think. He could get nowhere in the music world until he changed his label. He called himself Englebert Humperdink. The rest is history. And what was that other guy—Harold Spencer, I think. He wasn't doing all that well until he changed his label to Conway Twitty.

Brent Biehl lived in the Detroit area until he bought the property on Lake Superior north of Paradise called Sheldrake—property that once boasted a huge sawmill and thriving town. Brent, a dreamer and inventor in the spirit of Tom Edison and Henry Ford, got to thinking that all those giant piles of sawdust were going to waste. It was a time of energy crisis and fuel shortages. Brent got a government grant and some private investments for research into a process to compress sawdust and remove its moisture to make a briquette.

So, the product was born. What to call it? He decided on "Milltown Loggettes." The bag labels said they were great for charcoal-like cooking, campfires and woodstoves.

That didn't work. After thousands of dollars in consultation with advertising experts, they concluded that his bags of loggettes had to have the look of the Kingsford brand charcoal bags. So, Brent went to a blue-white bag and a new label: "Milltown Hardwood Briquettes."

That worked a little but not enough. So, another label change came: "Milltown Woodfire."

Suddenly, there was interest for the product in Japan,

but Japan's marketing experts said "Milltown" gave the image of a large, industrial city like Pittsburgh. Fact is, Milltown was intended to give the image of an Upper Peninsula ghost town that once had a sawmill.

Back to the label drawing boards. Now, the bag of loggettes says: "Woodfire, Made in the U.P. in a little Yooper Town on Da Shore of Da Big Pond."

Will it work? Who knows? Look what happened to Englebert Humperdink.

Brent also came up with a kitty litter product made of waste sawdust.

With no expensive consultations and no advertising executives, Brent simply called it "Kitty Cover." It's done quite well.

Say, Brent, I have a great idea for immediate public acceptance. Just call 'em Englebert Twitty Loggettes.

Christmas Past

November/December 1995

This is a time of year when families sit around recalling their most unforgettable Christmases. Our family does that, too. For me, it's easy—an indelible memory of a Christmas in Lansing 17 years ago.

It started great. My son, Steve, flew home from Denver where he was attending an auto repair school. Linda, a junior at Michigan State University, was also home. For my wife, Darl, and me, that was special. Those kids are our life.

A day or two after Steve arrived home, I was in my basement workshop tinkering when he came up behind and grabbed me in a playful father-son wrestling session. When I turned to look at him, I saw tears in his eyes. "I miss you, Dad," he said. I never heard four greater words.

Christmas does that. It's a time for families to reunite and fight lumps in throats.

Then things went downhill. Christmas Eve came and Linda became ill. Desperate, we took her to a hospital emergency room. As we waited with a long line of sick and injured people, Steve, Darl and I spent several restless hours. A man sitting next to me began to cry. I offered him comfort and asked what was wrong. "I just brought my mother here," he said, "she is old and she has severe stomach pains. This is Christmas Eve and, well, on Christmas Eve last year, my father died. God save us from another Christmas like that," he sobbed.

My heart went out to the man and as I wiped tears of my own away, I heard the wail of sirens from an ambulance. Steve and I watched as the paramedics rushed a man on a stretcher into the emergency room. They were frantically thumping on his chest. "Heart attack victim, cardiac arrest," said one of the office workers.

Time passed and a doctor called me to an examining room with Linda. "You'll have to take her to Sparrow hospital. She has an infection and a fever, we'll have to admit her and do some tests," he said.

"Wow. There goes Christmas," said Linda through tears. There were four glum faces in the Hough family as we got ready to leave.

As we put on our coats, a doctor called several members of another family waiting there. "He's gone," the doctor told the family, "we did all we could." It was the heart attack victim. The sobs of that man's daughters, son and wife will live with me forever.

Suddenly, Linda's problem seemed so minor. Surely, by comparison, they were. She spent Christmas Eve in the hospital and we were depressed. But a happy note was sounded in the morning when doctors told us she could go home. Suddenly, it was like other Christmases. We were around the tree in the living room by the fireplace opening gifts. Happy time had returned.

But there was one more Christmas downer in that 1978 year for Steve and me. We went to keep our noon appointment at the volunteers where we annually helped deliver hot Christmas meals to the elderly and shut-ins. We were given the name of an elderly woman living alone on Lansing's northeast side.

Steve and I knocked at her door for the longest time before we heard movement inside. After some time, we saw her open the door to peer out. We saw the reason for her slow movements. Using her walker and wearing an old flannel shirt that used to belong to her husband, she opened her door.

We told her we were delivering a hot Christmas meal from the Volunteers of America. Pride straightened her tiny, bent shoulders and she protested. But Steve and I convinced her to take the meal. We laid it out on the kitchen table and we prepared to leave. We said "Merry Christmas" and turned to go.

She looked at us for a moment and then broke into tears. Although my reporter efficiency was never at a lower level than at that moment, I still recall some of what she said. It went like this:

"Oh, I hear about Merry Christmas so often this time of year but Merry Christmas are empty words for me. There can never be a Merry Christmas for me ever again. New Years Eve is the worst for me because that's when my husband died. I had him for 53 years. There is nothing to live for now. I can't even do my own vacuuming. My home is a mess. I have no relative here. The next thing I fear is that I will lose my home to the government. I can't pay the taxes anymore. I don't think they care about old people anymore. I called several churches and other places to get a ride to my doctor appointment. No luck. I had to cancel it. I didn't have the money to pay the taxi fare or the doctor bill," she said.

On several occasions, I urged her to sit down and eat her meal before it got cold. But it soon became obvious to Steve and me that the meal was unimportant to her. Far more important was our visit on that Christmas day. Steve and I stayed and, although her meal got cold, we learned a lot about what it means to be old and alone.

We hardly spoke as we returned home. I felt bad, afraid I had overdone my do-gooder role and brought a special depression to my son's Christmas.

"Sorry, son, we have had a lousy Christmas this year," I said, as we parked our car in the garage.

He paused a long moment before he responded. "Well, we sure saw the other side of Christmas, didn't we Dad? I mean Christmas is not always merry is it? I don't think I'll ever forget that old lady," he said.

"Our family is awfully lucky, dad," Steve said as he shut the car door.

"Amen," I said.

Will Jim Regret This Column?

May/June 1996

My long career as a newspaper columnist has put me in front of hundreds of audiences for speeches. That public speaking element of my career came under discussion with *Country Lines* readers at a recent annual meeting of an electric co-op.

"How many speeches have you given?" one asked. I guessed two or three speeches a week for the nearly 30 years at the *Lansing State Journal* and at least a hundred in the past 10 years for the state's electric cooperatives.

But the next question left me uneasy. I wanted to dodge it because the honest answer was a bit embarrassing. The question was: "What's the most unusual speech you ever gave?"

So, after a very long pause, I answered. It was some years ago when I was doing a daily column for the *Lansing State Journal*. I was invited to speak to a large convention of Catholic nuns and priests. But the guy who introduced me there that day wiped me totally out before I ever got to the microphone.

Frank Hand, a longtime colleague and friend, introduced me to that group with these words: "Our speaker today is Jim Hough. He is a former whorehouse inspector and processor of afterbirth."

Frank then sat down and left me to explain myself to that religious group.

I could have killed him. But what could I do? I tossed away my prepared speech and began a reluctant explanation of how and why I inspected whorehouses and processed afterbirth.

The whorehouse part came when I served with the U.S. Army in Panama. Prostitution was legal in that country. They hung out a shingle just like a doctor or lawyer. "House of Love," the signs said. However, it was a strong violation of U.S. military rules for any soldier to enter one of those places.

So, when a soldier showed up at the medical dispensary with a venereal disease, my job was to interrogate him and try to get an identification of the infected woman involved. Armed with those descriptions I would set out with a Panamanian government official— each of us armed with a .45 caliber pistol—and attempt to find the woman. If we found her, the Panamanian government arrested her and forced her to get treatment for her disease. Good grief, what a job that was. I got kicked, scratched, bitten and mauled more than once. It was truly a sad situation there—so many women with no other way to feed their children. One Panamanian official told me that Panama City led the world's cities in venereal disease rates. I don't doubt it.

Okay, so how did I get to be a processor of afterbirth? Well, after the military service, I returned to Lansing where I got a job as a laboratory technician at the Michigan Department of Health laboratories.

I worked in the blood plasma unit, one of only two places in the world that manufactured anti-hemophilic serum needed so desperately by hemophiliacs, and we also manufactured anti-measles vaccine.

A large quantity of blood was needed for that project, so the state entered into a contract with the American Red Cross to collect afterbirth from Michigan's hospitals. The placentas, heavily supplied with blood, were frozen following the births and stored for later delivery to the state blood lab. At that time, there were more than 80,000 births per year in Michigan. It was an enormous task to process all that blood.

In the program's infancy, we had to do it all by hand—

extracting the blood into giant stainless steel vats. The program still goes on today, but the blood is removed from the placenta with far more efficient and computerized equipment.

Yes, yes, yes, I was an inspector of whorehouses and I did get a job as a placenta squeezer. I will always hate Frank Hand for that introduction. I feared all those Catholic nuns would be aghast with that earful. Instead, they said it was "one of the most interesting speeches ever heard."

So there, the secret is out. I'll probably regret this column for a long, long time.

Mad Call Disease

July/August 1996

It has taken years, but I recently solved the mystery of the mad caller.

A daily newspaper columnist is a favorite target of the anonymous caller. Some callers are sad, some funny, some angry, and many offer political commentary.

"I'm not going to give my name because you might put it in the paper," the callers say.

There was a month-long period in the *Lansing State Journal* newsroom about 10 years ago when my colleagues gravitated to my desk each morning as I turned on my telephone answering machine. "We want to hear what the mad caller has to say about you today," they observed.

Almost everyday, the mad, anonymous caller used a disguised voice to leave a message for me. Here are some I remember:

▲ "Yes, Mr. Hough, you have been selected for the city's beautification committee. Your assignment is to stay out of sight."

▲ "Yes, Mr. Hough, this is the Outer Space Travel Agency. We have your application for outer space travel but, after looking at your picture, we rejected it. We don't want to give alien life the wrong impression."

▲ Yes, Mr. Hough, this is Ringling Brothers Circus. We have an opening for a clown and we have chosen you--not because you are funny, but because of the way you dress."

Sometimes the mad caller was not bent on personal attack and merely left observations, such as:

▲ "What do you get when you cross the Atlantic with the

Titanic? Halfway."

▲ "What do you get when you lean a corpse against a doorbell? A dead ringer."

▲ "Why did the woman refuse to let doctors operate on her husband? She didn't want anyone opening her male."

It wasn't fun to be the Rodney Dangerfield of the newsroom--no respect. But there was always a slight hint of recognition when I heard that voice. Now, the mystery is solved.

It was Charles D. Mefford, who was then owner of WITL radio station in Lansing.

Charlie, a longtime friend and loyal supporter of my column, has a great sense of humor but he loves to terrorize me now and then. In a recent phone conversation, he slipped into the voice of the mad caller. Ahh ha! I had him. Mystery solved. After all those years.

Charlie and his wife, Diane, are now retired and dividing their time between Lansing and Florida's Angel Island.

He hasn't changed. Thank goodness.

My Age Of Wisdom

March 2002

I have sort of ignored my birthdays for 20 years. I purposely put them low on my worry list ever since that day I turned 50. Now, I have a new trauma—age 70. Good grief, where has the time gone?

No future birthday can ever equal the one I had at 50. That was the big one. Digging around in an old file, I found a column I wrote for the *Lansing State Journal* when I had the big five-zero. It read, in part:

My 30th birthday deeply depressed me. I thought I was over the hill, my youth was all spent.

My 40th birthday was a bigger trauma. I almost needed a psychiatrist's couch. I figured I was only a day or two away from retirement. That "life begins at 40" line didn't help. I was in shock.

Now, it's the big one, the really, really big one. I'll be 50 this month. And don't give me any of that "fifty is nifty" baloney, either. I'm practically on Medicare, only a breath away from Social Security. I never felt so old.

So, I decided to do something to kick myself out of the age doldrums. I'm holding a surprise birthday party for myself. I put a notice on the newsroom bulletin board. I'm telling everyone that gifts are perfectly in order and that I'm registered at Schmidt's Party Store, Mt. Hope Party Store, Alvarado's Party Store, Logan Center Hardware, Sears and Story Oldsmobile.

I have just checked every mouthy source I know in the newsroom and I still have not turned up a rumor about a gift committee being formed. I sure hope I don't get any gag gifts. An Olds 98 or two weeks in Hawaii would be nice. No, on second thought, two days in Paradise would be better than two weeks in Hawaii. After that comment, you'll think I'm already senile.

My surprise birthday party got way out of hand. Word spread beyond the newspaper, and about 200 people showed up at my home on that March 30, 1982. In the crowd were community dignitaries, many friends and colleagues. Lansing's leading TV station even brought it's evening news show to broadcast from my basement recreation room. What a wild night. I was almost over my depression at becoming 50 that night when I heard a live broadcast over the Grand Ole Opry station WSM in Nashville, Tennessee. Earlier, I had invited my longtime friend, Whispering Bill Anderson of the Grand Ole Opry, to the party. Bill sent me a telegram saying he could not attend because he was scheduled to perform. He said he loved me even though I was getting old, and he asked me to tune in to the Opry that night.

So, there we were, all those party guests and me, huddled around a portable radio as Bill Anderson told of his dear friend in Lansing hitting age 50. Bill introduced Opry old-timer Jumping Bill Carlisle to sing a song for me. Jumping Bill then sang his old hit song, "Too Old To Cut The Mustard Anymore." Some honor. I have news for those guys. Hank Williams didn't have to jump or whisper to be a Grand Ole Opry star.

* * * * *

My wife, Darl, found a column written on my 50th birthday. She demanded I reprint that here, too. With great humility, honor and embarrassment, I will grant her wish. My newsroom colleagues decided to shake me up with a surprise guest column. They designated Mark Nixon to write it. Mark's column read:

Jim doesn't know about this, and if he did, he would

probably give it the Onlooker Ax. Jim likes surprises as much as he likes hockey and the opera, which isn't at all. But I had the editors' permission to write this surprise Onlooker. More than that, I had their blessing. So Jim, do what you always do when something goes wrong—blame it on the editors.

You see, today is Jim Hough's 50th birthday. It's the same birthday he lamented in an earlier column; the same one he threw a surprise birthday party for. That's right, he hates surprises so much that he scuttled any surprise by throwing a party for himself.

And what a party it was. There was a bagpiper (Jim hates bagpipes) and a little guy in a tutu (I'm not sure how he stands on tutus). There was also a special dedication from his good friend, country music star Bill Anderson. The dedication came over Nashville's Grand Ole Opry station, WSM. It was 12:30 Sunday morning, and there was Jim with his ear to a portable radio listening to the song dedicated to him: "Too Old to Cut the Mustard."

But this column isn't to poke fun at Jim's advancing age. This column is about youth. All of us, at one time or another, go chasing after the fabled fountain of youth. Some of us—if we get lucky or wise enough—stop looking elsewhere and find youth lies closer to the heart than the date on a birth certificate. I once knew a man who died young, although he was 67. I know others under 40 who have all but given up on life's promise, and are very, very old.

Nobody owns the secret of being young, nor can they pass it on to a friend. But when you meet someone with that secret, you just know it. Meeting Jim for the first time or the 1,000th time, you just know it.

Jim's party last Saturday was not to celebrate his 50th birthday. It was to celebrate his youth. He is the youngest 50-year-old I know.

It is no accident that when young reporters begin work at the *Lansing State Journal,* many are drawn to the desk in the corner of the newsroom where Jim sits. It is no coincidence that some of the younger people in the newsroom suggested a surprise Onlooker to honor him today.

And, it is no accident that many of his faithful readers are of retirement age. They find in his column a youthful vigor that seems to shout, "Hey world! I'm alive and kicking!" They find, perhaps, a promise of a better day; not tomorrow, but right now, today.

Sounds like I'm putting the guy on a pedestal, right?

Right. But you should know that Jim never wanted a pedestal higher than a soapbox, where he could stand and say something encouraging about his fellow man, or maybe needle us about our follies. That's not such a terrible pedestal to endure, is it?

There were tons of people at Jim's surprise party Saturday. A lot of people hugged him, because they truly love the man. There was also, maybe, the unconscious wish that some of his youthfulness would rub off.

Too old to cut the mustard? How are you going to convince a kid from the U.P. of that?

Thanks, Mark, for that high praise 20 years ago. After 40 years and more than 9,000 columns, I feel my typing fingers worn down to the first knuckle. But, as Garfield said, there may be wrinkles on my face but none on my heart. My aim is to stay as youthful as I can, in spirit, until my last breath.

Treasured Friends

October 2002

Please don't think I'm a name dropper, but I can't resist telling a couple of stories about two famous friends of mine—Whispering Bill Anderson of the Grand Ole Opry and George Kell, baseball hall of famer. One story is inspirational, the other is sad.

Let's start with Bill Anderson. This story will help you understand why I love him so much. I was with Bill in Nashville recently to help him celebrate 40 years on the Grand Ole Opry. While there, it was announced that he would be the next inductee to the Country Music Hall of Fame. For Bill, that was the ultimate honor.

So it was natural for the press, TV and radio folks to spend a lot of time interviewing him and asking about his favorite songs, favorite people, and his greatest thrills.

Bill confessed to me that he couldn't tell about his greatest thrill in nearly a half-century in the music business because he feared it would come off as a bragging session. But I got it out of him...

Bill told the story of his greatest thrill in the music business something like this:

"In July 2000, I received a phone call from a man in Iowa who explained that his father, living out near Phoenix, was dying of cancer. He wanted to know what it would cost to have me go out there and perform for his dad in his home for a few minutes. He said I was his dad's favorite performer and it would mean the world to him.

"So I found myself suggesting he send me two plane tickets, one for me and one for Les Singer, my bandleader for the past 20 years. Les and I performed at the Saturday night Opry and then boarded a plane for Phoenix.

"They picked us up at the airport and took us to the old gentleman's home. He had no idea we were coming. He was there in his pajamas watching TV. He was shocked and could not believe I was there. He said he had just watched me on TV back at Nashville the night before. Les and I tuned up our guitars and we asked him what he'd like to hear. We then did his requests. It was all supposed to be an hour or so and then we'd go back to the airport. But we didn't leave that home until near midnight. We ate sandwiches and Les and I performed more music than we had in years. But it was surely one of the most magical days of our lives. It ranks as my biggest thrill in the music business—just to put a smile on that man's face. It clearly reminded me of the power of music and how it can touch us all in a special way. The old man died a few months later and his son said I had great impact on his dad.

"That old man will never know the impact he had on Les and me," Bill said.

The character of many entertainers would be vastly improved if they spent time around the great Bill Anderson. I have always been proud to call him a friend.

* * * * *

Now to George Kell. Readers of this magazine know all about Kell and his half-century as a Detroit Tiger third baseman and baseball broadcaster—now in the Hall of Fame. George's picture once graced the cover of this magazine because of his long devotion to rural electric cooperatives in Michigan and his home state of Arkansas.

I received a letter from George recently in which he told of his life's worst tragedy. He said he was alone at his home when he smelled smoke. He went upstairs and found the entire upper floor afire. He was overcome by smoke, but neighbors rescued him. Lost in the fire were all of his baseball memorabilia, trophies and honors. The worst was the loss of his collection of hard cover diaries he had kept over his long baseball career.

"I wanted them all to go to my children someday. Losing that collection of daily entries over a 20-year baseball and 30-year broadcasting career really hurt bad," he wrote.

Whenever I think about Kell and Anderson, I recall an incident in our friendship about 15 years ago.

George called me to say: "My God, Jim, you'll never believe it. I went to Nashville for a convention and I was leaving the airport when I saw Bill Anderson walking across the parking lot. I had never met him but I always loved his music. So I ran to stop him and asked if he was Bill Anderson. He knew who I was. In fact, he knew everything about me. We discussed you for several minutes and then Bill took me in his car to my hotel. He had me sign a ball for his son. What a thrill it was to meet Bill Anderson," Kell said.

A few days later, I got a call from Bill Anderson. "You'll never believe it, Jim, I got to meet George Kell. I ran into him at the airport. What a thrill that was for me. We talked about you a lot," Bill said.

No, this is not a name-dropping column. Instead it is a perfect reminder that famous people can be very warm and special. I have long treasured Bill and George.

I Love My Fishin' Buddy

July/August 2003

Every fisherman needs a fishing buddy. Mine is a girl. Well, she used to be a girl. For the past 46 years, she has been my wife.

Darl and I have had an amazing spate of fishing stories to tell. Best of all, they are true stories. All that despite the T-shirt she wears which says, "I fish. Therefore I lie."

Darl grew up fishing with her father, and I grew up living next to a brook trout stream in the Upper Peninsula. When we went on our honeymoon, we loaded up fishing gear and headed to Canada and the mouth of the Montreal River. We caught big, beautiful rainbow trout in those rapids. My oh my, the splendor of such a life—a honeymoon and fishing combination. Life was good.

I recall a time later when we were fishing at the mouth of the Tahquamenon River at Paradise. In the boat with us was our two-year-old son, Steve. Darl hooked onto a monster northern pike. She battled it and battled it. We finally got a look at it. I thought it was a fence post. What a monster—probably well over 30 pounds. About that time, Steve leaned over the boat to take a look and Darl's mother instincts replaced her fishing instincts. She reached to pull Steve back. The big pike ran. Before Darl could get control of her reel, the fish broke the line. Gone was the trophy monster. There was silence in our boat for a half hour. Steve is 43 now and Darl still lectures him about that fateful day when he cost her the big fish.

In that same river a few days later, we had not had much luck and were about to quit for the day. I stood up in the boat and flung a cast with a daredevil bait as far out toward the lake as I could. The bait soared and a seagull dove at it. The line became entangled with the bird. The gull flew away. I released the drag on the reel, not wanting to hurt the poor bird. But the flight brought the end of the line and a big jerk on my rod. The daredevil fell free from the bird. With a big measure of relief, I began to reel in. Suddenly, wham, a big strike. Once again, it was a monster. We finally reeled that one in—a 20 pounder. I had to give the seagull an assist.

Then there was the winter ice fishing. Darl loved to do that. We had a winter fishing shanty (we made it out of thin sheeting from casket crates we got from a Mt. Pleasant funeral home) and we loved to sit in there with our little heater and spear northern pike.

We had a live sucker decoy. We named him Harold and we put a weight on the line down there. When Harold drew a pike to the scene, we speared it. Well, we sat there one winter day when Darl was 7 months pregnant. She was bundled up in my hunting suit and barely fit through the shanty door. As we watched Harold swimming around down there, we saw a mean muskrat swimming after Harold. Quickly, I threw the spear and it nicked the muskrat in the rump. Angered, I guess, he came right up into the shanty. Believe me, you don't want to be in such a location with a cornered and angry muskrat. I opened the door and squeezed Darl out of there. I dove out behind her. We figured the rat could have that shanty all to himself and he could eat Harold, too, for that matter. But the critter dove back into the hole and swam away. Harold survived. Darl said it was time to go home. We did.

In recent years, we have been celebrating our August anniversary by taking our travel trailer on a trip to Canada for a wilderness fishing trip 400 miles north of our home. We always catch a lot of fish and enjoy the evening campfire where we get reacquainted again after a busy summer and a lot of company.

As we troll for northern pike and walleyes, we often get hold of big fish in that Canadian lake. That's when Darl's personality changes abruptly. She gets a big fish on the line and starts yelling at me to get the net. Soon, she has the big fish near the boat to be netted. But there is one big problem: I have severe visual impairment and I can't see the fish to net it. I make several desperate swaths at the critter. Meanwhile, Darl is coming apart.

"You net that fish next try or you'll be walking to shore," she yells. Good grief, Darl, there is 40 feet of water down there. What's this walking to shore threat? Finally, I get the fish in the net and drop it in the bottom of the boat. Then we look at each other and burst into laughter. For her, the laughter is the thrill of catching the fish. For me, the laughter is relief that she didn't throw me overboard. It's a real circus when we each get a fish on at the same time. Her fish has to be netted first. Otherwise, I fear she'd have a nervous breakdown.

But this past August, on our 46th anniversary and on my first cast of the fishing trip, I caught a northern pike 43 inches long and weighing 30 pounds. It was our biggest ever. Darl finally got it in the net, but she couldn't lift it into the boat.

At that lake, the rules say all fish over 34 inches have to be thrown back. Fortunately, we had the camera aboard and Darl shot some great pictures. Otherwise, nobody would have believed that story.

We spend three winter months in Texas on the Gulf of Mexico and have daily fun surf fishing. The day Darl caught a 20-pound Red Drum was her highlight.

But it is more than fishing fun when you do that kind of stuff with your wife. Despite her threats to throw me overboard, our fishing buddy relationship has been a vast marital enrichment.

The King Of Christmas Lights

November/December 2003

Neighborhood competition for the most unusual Christmas decorations is an American tradition. But I fear my neighbor has gone a bit too far.

About four years ago, I was outside stringing Christmas lights on my pine trees when I spotted my neighbor, Ben Musielak, in his yard. We are good friends and exchange good banter. So, I yelled to him.

"Hey, Ben, is this Christmas going to be like all others—with me carrying the entire neighborhood load for decorations? Are you going to be a Scrooge again this year?"

Amid his silence, Ben disappeared into his garage. I saw him come out with an axe and head into our nearby swamp forest.

First, you have to know that Ben is an intelligent, creative and inventive guy. He is a fireman and emergency medical technician at Sault Ste. Marie and he is a licensed builder of beautiful homes in his spare time.

About an hour later, Ben's wife, Debbie, called to say: "My God, Jim, what have you done to Ben? I think he has gone crazy. Look out your window. He is going out into Lake Superior with a tree on his back."

We dug out our binoculars and looked out into our front yard—which is, of course, Lake Superior. There was Ben in his waders and with all kinds of apparatus hung over his shoulder.

First, he placed a large plastic pipe into the icy water. Then he cranked up a gas-operated jet pump. He then jetted that pipe down into the Lake Superior sand. Then he stuck the trunk of the tree into the pipe. Then he returned to shore, leaving that tree about 300 feet out there in the lake.

As I stood there watching from my living room window, darkness came. Suddenly, WOW! That tree exploded with beautiful Christmas lights. I couldn't believe it. Ben had strung 300 feet of wire out there.

As I watched, mouth open in amazement, my phone rang. I answered and heard Ben say: "There, rotten neighbor, top that." He hung up.

No way. He wins. Now the tree is a tradition and folks living along the Superior shore enjoy it immensely.

Each spring, of course, Ben has to retrieve all that tree and wire apparatus from the melting ice. I have been hoping some governmental official would come and arrest him for lake pollution or something. That way, I'd have the last laugh. But I admit that I'd miss Ben's annual tree production and the beautiful results.

Now it has become quite a show when Ben heads out into the lake each year to set up the tree. Word spreads along the shore and he has quite an audience. One neighbor, Arnold Mills, even shoots bottle rockets out there to ruffle Ben's feathers a bit.

The best was last year. Ben had an audience as he dragged a big tree to the frozen shore. It was near zero degrees. Ben was in his heavy clothes and waders and wearing a bright orange stocking cap. None of us thought about getting a picture. We just watched in amazement. This time, we feared for his life.

With large, freezing waves crashing on the shore, Ben got his aluminum canoe. He placed the tree into the canoe. Then he attached his 300-foot reel of electrical line to the canoe. He got his plastic pipe AND HIS JET PUMP. Out into the lake he went.

As we all watched, nothing happened. The water in the jet pump froze. Back to shore comes Ben. Soon he emerged from his garage carrying a lighted propane torch and waded back out to the canoe.

While thawing out the pump with the torch, he ignited the tree. He jumped back from the blaze only a moment. Soon, he was splashing water into the canoe and he killed the tree fire. His fellow firemen would have been proud of him.

About that time, the electrical line detached from the canoe and fell into the lake. We all feared Ben would then be electrocuted and thus ruin Christmas for Debbie. Undaunted, Ben reached down into the lake and retrieved that electrical line.

Battling the waves, he soon had the tree stuck into the pipe and BINGO—the beautiful tree lights blazed.

We all applauded, but Ben heard nothing but the howling winds and waves as he wearily made his way back to shore.

I'm more compassionate than you might think. I went over there with a shot of brandy for him.

And so goes our life on the shore north of Paradise—where Ben is still the king of Christmas lights.

Caution: Do *not* try to copy Jim's neighbor. Always employ a licensed electrician when working around water.

Venison Is A Gift Of Love

November/December 2004

I can no longer resist telling the story about the blind guy who got his deer every year for 40 years.

Who is the blind guy? Me. What's more, I never fired a shot and it was not road kill.

I can no longer resist telling the story because it all speaks so well to the friendship, loyalty and dedication of my friends in law enforcement.

Ralph Waldo Emerson once said: "I didn't pick my friends. They were a gift from the good Lord."

This story of the annual deer coming to my home ready for the freezer began about 40 years ago when I was lying in a hospital bed in Mount Pleasant. I had been admitted there for some testing because I was losing my sight. The forecast was that I would become totally blind.

As I lay there one afternoon, pretty depressed, about 10 cops from the State Police and Mount Pleasant City Police surrounded my bed. They heard the bad news and wanted to visit me. But the conversation was difficult. Nobody knew what to say. Then, one burst into tears and said: "Well, damn it, Jim, you'll always have venison."

That remark came because I had gained a reputation for years with those guys on hunting and fishing trips where I was the only non-cop in the camp. We always cooked up venison and I loved it so much that I always pigged out and earned their kidding.

So, every deer season after that day in the hospital, the cops brought a deer to my home. They took turns. I learned later that they had a pact: Jim Hough gets the first deer that any of us shoots.

For the past several years, the deer was shot and delivered to me by Earl Johnson, retired commander of the Michigan State Police Post at Newberry.

I thanked Earl and asked him why he does that.

"Don't worry about it, Jim. It's my assignment," he said.

All of this is a bit unusual because the press and police are often in adversarial roles. Reporters demand facts that cops are often reluctant to release. But a reporter gets to know a cop's point of view pretty well when he sits in the other end of a fishing boat with them as much as I did as a young reporter.

When I wrote a daily column for 30 years in Lansing, I never missed an opportunity to show the average cop for what he is: A dedicated, caring person who is just like the rest of us. He wants to make his car and house payments, and he wants to have an orderly society with safe streets for his children. Many reporters didn't think it was much news when a cop risked his neck for some citizen or when he helped the little old lady change a flat tire. But I thought that kind of thing needed to be shared with the reading public. I never missed a chance to do that, and the cops appreciated it.

When I retired, more than 1,000 people attended a banquet at the Lansing Civic Arena. More than 200 of them were cops. They gave me lavish gifts and a special plaque and citation from the director of the Federal Bureau of Investigation.

I don't tell all this to brag. The ego went out of it for me years ago. I tell it because it says so much about what real cops are all about.

Some of them won't like me telling this story about my venison. Sorry, men, I know you prefer to be anonymous with your kindness, but this has simply gone beyond your private pact to remember Jim Hough. It has, at least in my mind, become a special story that had to be told.

In early December each year, about 300 cops gather for a luncheon at the Eagle Lodge in Lansing. They call themselves the Keystone Cops. They have been doing that for nearly 30 years. They said they got tired of meeting at funerals and started the annual luncheon. For the past 27 years, they have invited me to be their speaker. In all of my long newspaper career, I have never been more honored.

I'd like to print the name of every cop who brought me a deer over the past 40 years, but that would ruin it for them. It is not just meat for the table—it is an annual package of love that puts me in tears. I love you guys.

My View

It's All In The Attitude— Graduation Attitude

July/August 1999

My long career as a daily newspaper columnist brought me many coveted honors and awards, and even a nomination for the Michigan Journalism Hall of Fame. But an honor on June 6 at the Brimley High School commencement ceremony touched me most.

My old high school gave me a beautiful trophy signifying the "Distinguished Alumni Award." How could you be more honored? Who wouldn't like to have his old school think of him that way? Wow! It put me in tears. And a standing ovation from the school's 38 graduating seniors added a lifetime memory.

But I came back down to earth when my grandson, David, asked: "Grandpa, what is an extinguished alumni?" Well, maybe "extinguished" is closer to the truth.

There is something so special about graduation ceremonies— particularly at small high schools. I have long believed that young men and women graduating from small Upper Peninsula high schools are a little bit better prepared to tackle the world. Yeah, I admit I'm quite prejudiced on that, but I think I can make my case.

During my days in Lansing, I became acquainted with

T.A. Foresberg, owner of a large construction company that held multi-million dollar contracts all over the country. He told me he often sought out employees from an area between Detroit and Mackinac City. "I ask for five references. If they are from the Upper Peninsula, I ask them when they can go to work," he said.

His assessment boiled down to one word: Attitude. His claim was that attitude had more to do with success and failure than all abilities combined.

I thought about Mr. Foresberg at that Brimley commencement. When school administrators first asked me to make a commencement speech, I declined. I have done a few of those over the years and I think seniors hate them. While some pompous college president or politician stands before those seniors and belches out platitudes about "the youth of today are the leaders of tomorrow" and "the torch is passed to a new generation," the seniors sit out there sweating in their caps and gowns, waiting for the speech to end so they can go to the party.

But I couldn't resist talking to them for a couple of minutes about attitude.

I told them about Detroit Tiger pitcher Denny McLain. His enormous ability took him to amazing heights as he won 30 games in one season—a major league record. While that great ability took him there, it was his attitude that took him down. Soon, he was in trouble with the Feds for tax evasion and openly showed disrespect for fans, his bosses and himself. Today, he sits in a federal prison.

A sportswriter friend of mine once wrote: "Denny McLain had a million dollar arm and a 10-cent attitude."

And I told Brimley's kids about the great Helen Keller. It was a change in attitude that made her one of the world's most famous people. Blind, deaf and unable to speak, Helen Keller was a young woman at the turn of the century in a small Alabama town. She constantly threw herself on the ground in a rage and exhibited impossible behavior. Then a woman named Ann Sullivan came into her life and set out to change Helen's attitude. Thus at the age of 24, Helen Keller had graduated from college with a degree in English. She began a writing career that made her loved throughout the world. She was the guest of kings. Her attitude had changed.

Just before her death, Helen Keller wrote: "Thank God for my handicap, for, through it, I found myself and my work."

And I remembered another good example of attitude as a vital ingredient in good leadership. I told the grads about a scene shortly after the Civil War in Richmond, Virginia. It was a Sunday in a fashionable, all-white church. As the time for communion came, a poorly dressed black man came from the back of the church and knelt at the altar for communion. The church's all-white patrons were shocked and murmured their disgust. Suddenly, a white, bewhiskered gentleman left his seat and went to the altar to kneel next to the black man. Quietly, all others followed. That bewhiskered gentleman was Robert E. Lee. Attitude. Attitude. Attitude.

By the time this column gets into print, high school commencements will be done for this year. But I recommend you attend one somewhere next June. Nothing will uplift your spirits more than to see and feel the hope and enthusiasm in those young people as they go forth to battle the world.

The 38 seniors at Brimley earned college scholarships valued at nearly $200,000 and some of the top students could hardly carry their many awards as they left the school gymnasium. I hope I helped them realize that the most important thing they carried from that school was their attitude.

I'm confident of their future.

Can The Tigers Make Memories In New Park?

March/April 2000

When the first crack of the bat is heard this spring amid all the hoopla in something called Comerica Stadium, I'll be thinking of old Tiger Stadium at the corner of Michigan and Trumbull in Detroit.

I can't help reflecting on that final day at old Tiger Stadium last fall—an emotional time for any Tiger fan. I don't want to be an old grouch about it, and I know we can revere the past without fearing the future. Nevertheless, they'll never convince me that great baseball traditions can be recreated in a place bearing a commercial name, $2-million executive suites, and supporting multi-millionaire infielders who bat .200.

There will be no Ty Cobbs, Hank Greenbergs, and Al Kalines there again. Today, a star player sells himself to the highest bidder each year and ends his career having played for several teams. About the time fans get to like him, he's gone.

Meanwhile parents can't afford to take their young families to the ballpark anymore. Stadium seats, parking, hotdogs and pop will cost a family of four well over $100 per game.

Maybe future generations can learn to tolerate all this commercialism, but I find it and baseball a bad mix. Today, radio broadcasters give commercials for everything happening on the field. "That was a Tuffy Muffler double play... This pitching change is brought to you by the Miller Brewing Company... That home run courtesy of Sir Pizza..."

If I were sports editor at a Michigan newspaper today, I'd tell my staff that the name Comerica will never appear in my news columns. I'd just call it "The Stadium" and not let somebody get all that free advertising by paying to put their name on the building.

That old Tiger Stadium had to go, I guess, and the new one will offer more comfort and all that. But the modern nature of the baseball business hurts a lot. As I talk with some old baseball friends—George Kell, Ernie Harwell, Dick MacAuliffe, John Hiller, and others, they all share my fear for baseball's future. As John Hiller said to me, "Today's players go to work in a three-piece suit, carrying a laptop computer and copy of the *Wall Street Journal.* They are all businessmen first and baseball players second."

I was extra proud of Ernie Harwell in the final Tiger Stadium ceremony last fall. He got the biggest standing ovation of all that night. I found myself in tears a few weeks later when I shared some of my old Tiger Stadium memories with Ernie.

My dad lived for a short time as a boy in that old Tiger Stadium neighborhood. He looked through knotholes in a fence there at Ty Cobb when it was called Bennett Field. In later years, Dad took me to many Tiger games. Oh, so many great memories! I recall my first lesson in sportsmanship came there one day as I sat in a packed stadium with my dad watching a double header with the Boston Red Sox.

When the first game reached the ninth inning, the Tigers had a one-run lead and the great Ted Williams strode to the plate for Boston with the bases loaded. The Tigers brought in a left-handed relief pitcher named Al Aber, who then struck Williams out. The packed stadium went crazy. We whipped 'em. Then came the second game, and it was almost another storybook ending. Once more, Williams came to the plate in the ninth with a chance to win the game. The Tigers again brought in Aber. "That's great, Dad, we'll get him out again," I said. My father smiled, hugged my shoulder, and said, "No, son, not twice." And the great Williams hit the first pitch into the right field second deck to win the game. I recall the silence of all those stunned fans. And then, every Tiger fan stood to give Williams a standing ovation. What an amazing display of good sportsmanship. He had just beaten us, but we all admired him as one of the greatest hitters of all time.

My son, Steve, reminded me of another touching moment when we sat in Tiger Stadium together. It was a game with the California Angels. In the pregame warmups, a ball rolled over to the wall in front of our box seats. As the player came to get it, Steve, then about 12, said: "Hey mister, how about giving me that ball?" The player smiled and said, "I need it right now, son, I'll give it to you later." But Steve doubted that very much.

After the "Star-Spangled Banner" was sung, the umpire yelled "play ball," and as the first Angels batter stepped into the box, a player came running out of the Angels dugout to whisper something to the home plate umpire. The ump called time, and the player ran to our box and handed Steve the ball. "I'm sorry son, I almost forgot," the player said.

That player was Alex Johnson, the American League batting champion that year. Johnson was often in the news as a baseball bad guy, but my son had a different perspective. "There is sure another side of Alex Johnson," said Steve. I agreed.

Yeah, so many great memories. Steve and I often went to the old stadium together for a whole weekend of baseball. We'd ride from Lansing on a train or bus and stay in a downtown Detroit hotel. We'd attend games on Friday night, Saturday and Sunday. My role as a newspaper columnist got us special privileges. Steve was occasionally invited to the Tigers locker room.

In 1968, there were special moments for me. The Tigers won the pennant, and I'll never forget my father's wide-eyed excitement as I took him with me to those games. In fact, my greatest thrill at the old stadium was those World Series games with my aging father. I watched his emotions spill into tears several times.

Gosh, I hope somebody feels that way about Comerica Stadium 80 years from now, but I doubt it.

Bagpipes Make Me Cringe

May 2001

I know I'm about to irritate all you folks of Scotch descent, but I think it's time I made a confession to readers who like honesty in their columnists.

Simply put: I HATE BAGPIPES!

There, it's out. I feel better. I don't know what it is about those squealy things, but it's like the scrape of fingernails on a blackboard. They send me scurrying to find my earplugs.

I recall years ago when the *Lansing State Journal* sent me to Alma to cover the huge, annual Scottish festival there. All those bagpipes marching in parades sent me right out of town. I got chewed out by my editors for bad coverage. I didn't care. I couldn't take it when all those bagpipes got cranked up to the sounds made by a wounded rabbit.

Knowing my allergy to bagpipes, some of my Lansing friends often terrorized me with them. Guys like Tom Shawver and Larry Oliver showed up with those things at my birthday parties and the like. Once, they even invaded the newspaper's newsroom. My colleagues applauded while I cringed.

The worst, though, came at my retirement party—a monstrous event at the Lansing Civic Arena. As nearly 1,000 persons cheered, I was ushered to the head table by Shawver and Oliver amid sickly sounds from bagpipes. YUK!

One of my longtime friends and former colleagues, Bruce Cornelius, recently sent me some great stuff that tell about bagpipes as they are. Thanks, Bruce, I loved every one of those little sayings. Heck, I'll share a few of them with you here.

Q. *What's the difference between a bagpipe and an onion?*
A. No one cries when you chop a bagpipe.

Q. *What's the difference between a bagpipe and a trampoline?*

A. You take off your shoes when you jump on a trampoline.

Q. *How is playing a bagpipe like throwing a javelin blindfolded?*

A. You don't have to be very good to get the people's attention.

Q. *What's the difference between a lawn mower and a bagpipe?*

A. You can tune the lawn mower.

Q. *If you were lost in the woods, who would you trust for directions: An in-tune bagpipe player, an out-of-tune bagpipe player, or Santa Claus?*

A. The out-of-tune bagpipe player. The other two indicate you have been hallucinating.

Q. *What's the definition of a gentleman?*

A. Someone who knows how to play the bagpipe and doesn't.

Q. *What's the difference between a dead snake in the road and a dead bagpiper in the road?*

A. Skid marks in front of the snake.

Q. *What's the difference between a dead bagpiper in the road and a dead country singer in the road?*

A. The country singer may have been on the way to a recording session.

Q. *What's the range of a bagpipe?*

A. Twenty yards if you have a good arm.

Q. *Why are bagpipers' fingers like lightning?*

A. They rarely strike the same spot twice.

Q. *How can you tell if a bagpipe is out of tune?*

A. Someone is blowing it.

Q. *Why do bagpipers walk when they play?*

A. To get away from the sound.

Q. *What's the definition of "optimism"?*

A. A bagpiper with a beeper.

The Real Weather Report

November/December 2002

"What's this ugly mess out there? I thought they said this would be a beautiful and sunny day," my wife, Darl, said as she awakened to see a cold and rainy morning.

"That's your trouble," I said, "you pay too much attention to those weather forecasts." That brought silence. Darl is sick of my lectures on that subject.

On the other hand, I'm kind of sick of the naïvetè the American public has in listening, watching and reading those weather forecasts with such rapt attention and confidence. I don't blame weather forecasters—private, governmental or otherwise. They are just doing their job as best they can. But the simple truth is that they are wrong, dead wrong, a large percentage of the time. Those of us who regulate our lives according to those forecasts have only ourselves to blame.

I recall when the National Weather Service office in Lansing was honored for having the highest accuracy rate in the state—80 percent. That's a good average, for sure, but we need to realize at the same time that they were dead wrong 20 percent of the time. That too is a high figure.

What gets me most are those private meteorologists hired by the TV stations. They bring more showmanship than accuracy to the scene. Each day, they tell us what the weather will be the next day and they do it with a special sound of authority. The next day on the air they present the new forecast with the same sound of authority—never pausing to say "by the way, folks, we blew it yesterday."

For more than 20 years, I wrote the daily front page weather forecast and story for the *Lansing State Journal*. In addition, the late Bob Babb, my close friend, was the chief meteorologist in charge of all forecasting for Michigan's lower peninsula. That gained a lot of insight for me. Weather forecasting is better because of modern-day technology, but I doubt those forecaster accuracy rates will ever get much above 80 percent. Not with Mother Nature out there smirking at them all.

Some folks blame the weather on God. I'm not sure about that anymore after a conversation I once had in downtown Lansing with Rev. Bill Hill, pastor of St. Paul Episcopal Church. It was a beautiful day, and I said to Bill: "Why don't you talk to the man in charge up there and get all days to be as nice as this one?"

Rev. Hill replied: "Don't get on my case, Jim, I'm in sales, not management."

In any case, I offer this simple piece of advice: Use the forecast as a guide, but don't ever let it regulate your life and your daily activities and plans.

Speaking of weather-related issues in our lives, I noticed several of my neighbors along our rural road putting up new mailboxes this spring. That's because those boxes were knocked down last winter by snowplows. My neighbors grumbled and cursed the plow drivers. I could not join in on that complaint. I recalled those days when I was a young lad growing up in the eastern Upper Peninsula and riding in a snowplow truck with my dad.

Dad was a state highway department employee responsible for plowing many miles of roadway. What I remember most was the blowing and drifting winds that made it nearly impossible to see anything on a roadside—especially something as small as a mailbox. My dad always stopped to apologize to the mailbox owner when he knew he had hit one of them, but there was nobody better at highway plowing than my dad, and he smashed his share of mailboxes. I tried to explain that to my neighbors, but it fell on deaf ears. Come on, you guys, mailbox replacement is part of a Yooper's life.

There is a growing problem, however, with destruction of mailboxes by ruthless vandals—mostly young folks who think it fun to drive through rural areas setting homemade bombs in mailboxes or driving by to slam them with a baseball bat.

Recently, I saw a rare sight—an angry Lee Talboys. Lee, a famed Lansing-area musician and longtime close friend, is always even-tempered. But he was livid as I talked to him.

"What's the matter, Lee, did Marge burn the homemade bread or something?" I asked.

"Naw, Jim, it's just those young idiots who think it is great fun to drive around smashing mailboxes. It's bad enough when snowplows knock them down, but when young people do it just for kicks—that's sick, just sick. I replaced by box four times in two months, and who knows how much mail I have lost. The boxes are expensive," Lee said.

Since that episode, Lee has given up. He drives to town every day to get his mail. He told me of one neighbor who had replaced her mailbox 12 times in two years.

What we need is far more effort to catch those vandals. Interfering with the U.S. Mail is a serious offense, and every one of those mailbox smashers need a jail cell and a psychiatrist, in that order.

The Dear Departed Deserve A Name

April 2003

"Don't you ever write anything serious?" a *Country Lines* reader asked recently.

So, I'm going to write a serious column. Funerals. How's that for a serious subject?

When you reach age 70, you have had a lot of experience at funerals. Fact is, you've probably been a pallbearer too much. But what bugs me most is the terrible, terrible rate of incompetence among the clergy at funerals.

Yeah, I know it is not the preacher's job to eulogize the person in the coffin and I know the clergymen feel they must use the occasion to preach hell and damnation for those of us who are about to die. But, Lord sakes alive, shouldn't the name of the dead person come up at some point in the ceremony?

I have attended a number of funerals in which the name of the person in the coffin never came up. In other ceremonies, the name of the deceased got only a minor mention. I insist that is preacher incompetence. Fire 'em.

Some years ago, I attended the funeral of a famous Associated Press writer, Bob Voges, in Lansing. The church was packed to the rafters. When the ceremony ended, Bob's name had never been mentioned. I was shocked. The next day, I called the pastor, himself a famous Lansing clergyman. "That's our church's practice and doctrine," he said, "We are there to honor God and not to talk about the dead person," he said.

"Well, Mr. Clergyman, it is time for you and your congregation to rise up and change those rules," I blurted angrily.

Like I said earlier, I know it is not the preacher's job to eulogize. But how can he go through such a ceremony without mention of why we are all there?

Some years ago, I was asked to be a pallbearer for Lionel Fairchild, a longtime craftsman who was an artist at stonework and carpentry. The preacher mentioned him briefly and observed that he was a carpenter and cement block layer. On the front of that church—still there today—was a giant cross, made of stones. It's among dozens of area landmarks created by that great man. I confronted that preacher after the ceremony. His response was: "Well, I didn't know much about him." That's incompetence, nothing less. He should have interviewed the family and learned something about Mr. Fairchild. Failing that, he should have been fired.

Perhaps the word "eulogy" is the problem. Some don't deserve a eulogy, I guess, but they do deserve some minor recognition of who they were and what they did and why someone loved them.

Some of you may have read the column I wrote last year when my beloved coach, Karl Parker, called me to his deathbed and asked me to speak at his funeral. For me, it was the greatest honor of my life and at the same time, my most difficult assignment. But Mr. Parker cautioned me this way: "Jim, I don't want a eulogy. This is not about my ego. It's just that I'd like to be able to say something to all those former students of mine. If you represented them at my funeral, you could say it for me," he said.

What could be more appropriate at the funeral of a legendary teacher and coach? Mr. Parker was a member of the Michigan Basketball Coaches Hall of Fame, the Upper Peninsula Sports Hall of Fame and the Brimley High School Sports Hall of Fame. Just to mention all that makes a eulogy of sorts, but his humble aim was to honor his students at his funeral. Good thing he didn't belong to the same church as Bob Voges of Lansing because they'd not even mentioned his name.

Guess by now you have detected that I'm a bit critical of incompetent clergy. Yet there are so many great clergymen who are smart enough to know that a funeral ceremony is a perfect place to make new friends and new converts. All it takes is a simple act of kindness to the audience that came out of respect for the dead, not out of respect for the preacher.

Every member of the clergy should be required to read a book written by a friend of mine, Kenn Filkins, editor of *The Sault Evening News*. Kenn, a longtime clergyman before he turned to journalism, wrote a book entitled, *"Comfort Those who Mourn—How To Preach A Personalized Funeral Message."*

Kenn's book, already through several printings, is widely used as a textbook in seminaries and bible colleges. Among the chapter headings is: "Getting Personal—interviewing the family."

Although Kenn's book is aimed at helping the clergy, it has deep thoughts and insightful material—good reading for all of us. You can contact him at *The Sault Evening News*, Sault Ste. Marie, MI 49783.

We all learn as we go along in life. Perhaps one of my biggest regrets came in connection with a funeral. Our family left Lansing to enjoy a weekend at our little cabin in Paradise. When we arrived in that tiny Upper Peninsula community, we stopped for gas. There on the gas pumps was a sign saying, "Closed for a funeral." When I checked on it, I found that the funeral was for the wife of the owner of the gas station. The owner of the station, Dick Waller, was a very good friend who had done me many favors.

But I didn't go to the funeral that afternoon because I didn't have a suit with me. I was clad only in old blue jeans. What a guilt trip that was. It ruined my weekend with the family. On Monday, I went back to work at the *Lansing State Journal* wearing a brand new suit I had purchased earlier. As I walked into the newsroom, one of my colleagues asked: "Hey, Jim, where are you preaching today?"

I sat down at my desk and I cried. Then I turned to my typewriter and wrote a column on the subject. Mostly, it was an apology to Dick Waller. Never again will I ever let my clothing keep me away from a friend in his time of grief.

Blind Man In The Women's Restroom

January 2004

As readers of this column know, I have been legally blind for over 40 years. That handicap has many times put me into the wrong restroom.

So many restrooms are in darkened hallways and the signs, *for various reasons,* are impossible for a partially-sighted person to see.

Whenever that happens to me, I hear a woman scream or ladies titter. That's when I say: "Sorry, I'm just here to fix the toilet."

One time, my wife, Darl, and I were in a beautiful restaurant in Toronto when I felt the urge. Some guy was being artistic and the labels above the doors were carved in the wood. One was supposed to say "Kings" and the other "Queens," but neither was clear to a blind guy. I walked in amid yells from two women. Quickly, I acted drunk. I staggered and slurred my words, made an apology, and got out of there.

Another time, I was visiting the Detroit Tigers in Lakeland, Florida, when Tiger pitcher John Hiller directed me to the restroom at the Foxfire Restaurant. On the door of the men's was a picture of Clark Gable. On the women's was a picture of Betty Grable. I went through Clark's door fully expecting it to be the women's biffy. It wasn't.

Bathroom signs may call for cleverness, but some folks go too far in their assumption that everyone has 20/20 vision.

Here are some other examples:

Dames and Dams. Pointers and Setters. Inboards and Outboards. Lads and Ladies. His and Hers. Guys and Gals. She and He. Men and Women. Johns and Janes. Cowboys and Cowgirls. GIs and WACs. Swabies and Waves. Flyboys and WAFs. Feminine and Masculine. Male and Female. Dolls and Hunks. Boars and Sows. Hens and Roosters. Bucks and Does.

Even in the right biffy, a partially-sighted person has a problem with signs. Towel dispensers might say "push here," but the blind guy can't read it and winds up walking out wiping his wet hands on his trousers.

I have learned to depend on my wife to say, simply: "Yours is on the left."

On behalf of the blind folks in Michigan, I took up a crusade about 20 years ago when I was a daily columnist in Lansing. I fought for state legislation to require Braille labels on public restrooms and elevators, along with curb cuts for those in wheelchairs. Guess what?! Legislators responded and I was given a Presidential Citation For Service to the Handicapped. It was issued by President Nixon and presented to me at a large Lansing banquet by former Gov. G. Mennen Williams.

I don't mention that to brag, but to point out the importance of a simple courtesy to the handicapped.

Now, let's move the blind guy into a restaurant. Here, he is handed a menu which he obviously cannot read, even in large print. So, he is a little embarrassed to have someone read it all to him out loud.

Therefore, they all do what I do. I order a hamburger or some other common item I know is on there somewhere.

I am reminded of the time my friend, Bob Babb, and I were on a fishing trip and stopped at a Gaylord restaurant. Bob could drive without his glasses, but he couldn't read a menu without them. So we had asked the waitress to read the menu. Seated next to us were two state police troopers who had to wonder a bit later as those two blind guys got into the car and drove off.

A blind guy wants some salt or pepper on his food. How does he tell which shaker? My technique is to shake the contents on the back of my hand. I can feel the salt hit, but not the pepper. And what about those little containers with butter and jam? They all have hidden little tabs you have to pull open. Impossible for the blind. Same is true for the crackers wrapped in plastic. I just rip'em open with my teeth (much to my wife's dismay).

Most restaurants, of course, go for atmosphere with candles or dim lighting. In there, the blind guy has a better chance for equality. But leaving a tip in those darkened places has often messed up my finances. To the partially-sighted, a $10 bill may look like $1, or a $20 bill like a $50 bill.

I went to lunch with a friend, and as we were leaving the parking lot a waitress came running out to stop us. "Sir, you left a $10 bill for a tip and I'm sure you meant it to be a $1 bill," she said.

"Yes, I intended it to be a $1 bill, but now I intend for it to be the $10 bill. I appreciate your honesty," I said.

I'm sure waiters and waitresses have often been flabbergasted at the tips I've left. Later, of course, I'd be going through my billfold and wondering whatever happened to that $10 or $20 I thought I had.

Longtime friends often forget my visual handicap and find themselves embarrassed. I try to relax them. That's the time for a good sense of humor. "Just call me cousin weak eyes," I say. I recall the time a buddy, Sam Corey, took me to the dog races in Florida. He handed me a copy of the racing sheet. "What will I do with that?" I asked. Sam started to explain that I needed it to handicap the races and then he realized I could not read it. He felt bad until I started to win every race by betting on the dogs with the strangest names. My biggest win came when I bet on a dog that had stopped to relieve himself just before the race. Sam loved to tell that story about my system of handicapping the dogs.

Once, Darl and I went to an oyster bar and they brought us a bucket with steamed oysters still in the shells. The technique for eating them was to stick a knife into the crack of the shell to pry them open. In order to see the crack I had to place the oyster shell up close to my eyes. With the danger of stabbing myself and putting up with the juices squirting in my eyes, I gave up. Darl had to do it. I heard a guy at the next table say, "Look at that lazy man. He makes his wife open those shells." Oh well, that's the life of a "cousin weak eyes."

Blindness can get a guy into deep trouble sometimes. Those stories abound in my case because I'm quite active and adventurous. I left my hotel room in Lakeland, Florida, to take a walk by nearby Lake Parker. Later, someone pointed out a big sign on the pathway: "Proceed beyond this point at your own risk because of reptiles." That gave me a shiver. They meant alligators.

Because I am always lost in parking lots, we now insist on owning bright red vehicles and that little remote that sounds the horn in our vehicle.

For many years, my sock drawer has contained socks of only one color—black. They always match. I let Darl pick out my ties.

I don't like museums where they have those little printed messages to tell about the exhibit. I just stay out in the car.

Darl is wonderful as we travel over the highways. She reads the road signs to me. I have enough vision to enjoy the scenery, but one always wonders what the signs say.

Gas pumps kill me. I don't like to have Darl pumping gas, so I do it. But the signs on the pumps—selecting the grade and amount of gas, or knowing which button to push for a credit card—make it impossible for a blind person. We just laugh it off, though. Darl pushes the buttons and I pump the gas.

Oh, those modern motel keys—plastic cards with careful instructions on how to insert them to open the door. I have spent up to 20 minutes fiddling with those things before I get the door open. By that time, my ice cubes have melted.

And another impossible task—reading price tags in the stores! Keeping a checking account? No way. Thank goodness for Darl.

I have learned to avoid buying something that has to be assembled. If it requires following directions, I'm a wreck. What should be fun turns into an ulcer.

Someday, I'm going to do myself in by taking the wrong medications. Wow! Now there's a real challenge for a blind guy. I wonder how many times I have taken my wife's thyroid medication thinking it was an allergy pill?

I love to play cards. My favorite game is euchre. I can still do it with the right set of friends who can remember to call out what card they turned up as trump. Best of all, I have a good excuse when I renege.

I have had to give up some things I love. In the army, I won a regimental championship playing pool. My daddy taught me the art of that game. But now I can't see the eight ball and the fun has gone out of it. Same is true of golf. I once got pretty good at that game. Now, I can't watch the ball in flight and the fun went out of it. Biggest frustration of all came when I had to give up brook trout fishing. Too many frustrating hazards of brush and snags for a blind guy. Can't see to put the monofilament line into the hook.

Some things I won't give up, though. I still go to baseball games, even though I can't follow the ball anymore. I just love the game and the baseball park atmosphere.

Ah, enough of all this. I have often seen the other side of blindness. It makes one appreciate things so much more. It always bothered me when one of my grandchildren crawled up in my lap with a kids book to say: "Grandpa, read me a story." It was always impossible to explain to a child about my vision problem. They saw me doing a lot of normal things and they could not understand my handicap. But then there always came the time when the child grew up and crawled up into my lap with the offer to read to grandpa. When my grandchildren felt it important to read something to grandpa, the lump in my throat grew large.

You Know You're Old . . .

February 2004

Bob Hope's death last year at age 100 was, for many of us, a time for reflection.

Bob once said he was so old that they had retired his blood type. When he was born, there were no cars, airplanes or television. Good grief! What a century he lived.

I got to thinking about my own life. Heck, I'm 73 and I don't feel old at all. Despite my attitude of youth, those years have seen some amazing things. I not only witnessed the development of television, a man on the moon, three big wars and computers, but it occurred to me that I was 16 before I lived in a house with an inside bathroom.

Recently, I bought a new, state-of-the-art wood stove for my Upper Peninsula home, and then realized I had worn out five other stoves in the past 50 years. And, I bought more than 25 cars, and....My-oh-my what a ride the 20th century has been for so many of us!

I remember a time about 25 years ago when I was dazzled by a bunch of old-timers in a discussion at a Lansing restaurant. There was a group of old men who met daily for coffee. They called themselves the "Remember When Club." I was about 45 and a daily columnist for the *Lansing State Journal*. I decided to sit in with those guys one day and take some notes. I later wrote a column listing some things those old-timers remembered in just that one-hour session way back then. I dug out that old column. It read, in part:

When a nickel bought two postage stamps and a postcard, too.

When mail was delivered to your home twice a day.

When cream popped the lid on the glass milk bottle.

When ice was delivered to your ice box according to the number of pounds indicated on a note in the window of your unlocked home.

When babies, not dolls, originated in the cabbage patch.

When one size didn't have to fit all.

When long underwear was put on for the duration.

When baseball was played on Sunday in the park and not every night in a living room.

When SWAK and PDQ (Sealed With A Kiss and Pretty Darned Quick) were the only acronyms you needed to know to be considered reasonably intelligent.

When plumbing meant a pail at the kitchen sink, a long rope at the well, and a long path—scary at night and slippery in winter.

When two pieces of string did not a swimsuit make.

When you went to school every day, regardless of snow depth and storms.

When there was neither electricity nor gas.

When carpets were laid out on the grass to get a clubbing from a rug beater.

When grass was a lawn and pot was a cooking container, and when coke was a drink.

Fact is, you wouldn't have to be very old to remember many of the above items.

When you are young, you hate it when your parents start talking about the good old days when they had it so rough. My daughter, Linda, and my son, Steve, used to get up and leave the room when I started on that stuff. I think I did the same to my parents. Like I said earlier, I still feel pretty darned young—at least in mind and heart—and I don't waller in the past much. Having said that, I remain perfectly amazed at the history lesson of the short 100 years of Bob Hope's life. Whew! What a ride it has been.

A friend of mine says he knows he is getting old because he gets exhausted dialing so many telephone numbers for a long distance call. It used to be one twist of a lever on the phone box and then, "Hi Sarah, ring the Smith house."

And, as all you rural electric cooperative customers know, electricity to the nation's rural areas only recently celebrated its 65th birthday.

Here are some other tips on aging:

When the gleam in your eye is from the sun hitting your bifocals.

When your little black book only has names ending in M.D.

When you get winded playing chess.

When your children look middle-aged.

When you finally make it to the top of the ladder only to find it placed against the wrong wall.

When you know all the answers but nobody asks you the questions.

When your knees buckle but your belt won't.

When you burn the midnight oil after 9 p.m.

When your back goes out more than you do.

When you have lots of room in your house, but none in your medicine cabinet.

When you sink your teeth into a good steak and they stay there.

The Center Of Things

March 2004

Although I never got high grades in my high school and college geography classes, I feel compelled to give a geography lesson to all southern Michigan newspaper editors and TV station news directors.

Their problem is that they don't understand "northern" and "southern" when they refer to towns in Michigan.

It bugs me that newspapers and TV stations in Detroit, Lansing, Flint and Grand Rapids refer to Mount Pleasant and Clare as "northern" Michigan communities. Balderdash.

The Clare Chamber of Commerce has long enjoyed referring to Clare as the "Gateway to the North." The fact is, a gateway to the north would have to be placed at Mackinaw City.

I'm tired of all those lower peninsula TV stations doing their nightly weather forecast shows with a map on the screen that ends at Mackinaw City. No "Yooperland" in our Michigan geography?

Some years ago, I was a *Lansing State Journal* reporter charged with covering Gratiot, Isabella and Clare counties. I received a news release from the St. Louis (Michigan) Chamber of Commerce proudly announcing that city as located exactly in the geographical center of Michigan. They put up big roadside signs to proclaim St. Louis as "The Geographical Center of Michigan."

Well, folks, when I got done writing several stories to remind St. Louis that Michigan had an Upper Peninsula, they were forced, in embarrassment, to take down those signs. They hated me, but I didn't care. Right is right and wrong is wrong. They were dead wrong.

Those of us who live in the eastern end of the Upper Peninsula have a nightly belly laugh watching Channel 10 TV present the evening news. Although the station has a Cadillac-Traverse City base, it proudly proclaims its coverage of us folks up here in Sault Ste. Marie, Newberry, St. Ignace, Paradise, Curtis and other eastern U.P. towns.

At least 30 times in their broadcasts, "northern Michigan" is in front of Mancelona, Clare, Alpena, Traverse City, Cadillac, Indian River, Grayling, Gaylord, and more.

Northern Michigan? Listen up now, all you news directors and editors. Pay close attention to this simple fact:

When you are in Mackinaw City, you are still in "central" Michigan.

Somehow though, I fear all this will go on deaf ears and your news reports of "northern" Michigan towns will remain a comedy show and not a newscast for those of us who live above the bridge.

It is terrible enough that most of us don't know where so many foreign countries are located, but it is a downright pathetic lack of geographical intelligence when we don't know anything about our own state.

We love all you "central" Michigan folks in Traverse City, Cadillac, Gaylord and Petoskey. We think you are concerned and intelligent folks. But all of you need to educate your news writers at Channel 10.

Time To Drop The Mexican Stereotypes

July/August 2004

This column may be a departure from my normal fare, but I think it is time for a discussion—gringo to gringo.

As most know, the Latino population in the United States has now passed that of African Americans. Call them Mexicans, Chicanos or Latinos; they are now the largest minority in this land.

What bothers me is a prevailing attitude, especially up north, that causes we gringos to think Mexicans are all criminals who crossed the Rio Grande River in the dark of the night to steal our cars and rob our homes.

That attitude is not shared by the millions of "Winter Texans" who spend the winter months in the Rio Grande Valley. They see the other side of the Mexican culture and they admire it.

We Americans could learn a lot from the Mexican culture—particularly family values. Consider this: In the entire country of Mexico, there is not one nursing home. If mom or dad becomes ill or too old, the sons and daughters take them into their homes. They are all in church every Sunday, and all things such as shopping and recreation are done together—as a family.

Despite that, too many of us gringos consider them as aliens – untrustworthy and criminal.

It is all about economics. Put me in their place with my family in an economic struggle for survival, and I might swim the Rio Grande River and brave the alligators and the border patrol—anything to help my family.

Their biggest trump card when they enter America—

legally or illegally—is their willingness to work, and work hard.

It is time we gringos shuck the images and stereotypes we gained from the old western movies where the fat Mexican bandit wore his cross-belts of ammunition and raided American farms and villages.

Winter Texans quickly get a new image of Mexicans. After all, if you draw a line east to west through the middle of Texas, everything south of that line was once Mexico. The population there is still solidly Mexican in culture. Spanish is still the language, but there is one difference northern gringos soon learn. When you point to a person in the Rio Grande Valley, you should not refer to them as Mexicans. The fact is that they are all U.S. citizens—and have been for as long as we have—and they are loyal Texas residents.

After six years of winter living among the Mexican people, I find them warm and neighborly. Try speaking a little Spanish, and they will quickly embrace you and help you.

When our vehicle needed a front-end alignment, we went to a small service station called Joe's Texaco. The owner, Dan Gulierrez, said he could do the job. When he finished, he feared there was a factory defect in our vehicle and urged us to have it checked by our dealer. We paid and left. Two weeks later, there was a knock on our door one evening. "Hi, Mr. Hough, I was just on my way home and I wondered how your wheel alignment is holding," said Dan, with a Mexican accent. "Before you go home to Michigan, let me check the alignment again so you won't wear out tires on your trip. I won't charge you," he said.

Raul Melquizo, owner of Las Dos Republicas, a nice restaurant in Matamoros, became a friend of ours. On our last visit there, I told Raul that I had been searching for the CD recordings of Charmin Chorrea, a Mexican guitarist. His music is so special, but I was unable to find it at stores. Raul left the restaurant and went to his home where he got three of the CDs. "You can't pay for them Jim, they are a gift to you and Darl," he said.

I could go on and on, but I tell those two little stories because they more accurately represent the nature of the Mexican people.

As a popular border town, Progresso gets thousands of visitors from America daily. Gringos go there for a wide variety of Mexican bargains, including dental care and drugs at one-third of the U.S. cost. In early April, tragedy struck that little Mexican town when a gas explosion wrecked several buildings and killed six people. Immediately, fire and rescue units from all the U.S. border towns sent help across the border. Winter Texans swung into action in big numbers to bring food and other support to the rescue workers. None of it surprised me; because we learned that kind of neighborliness from our neighbors to the south.

Author's note: Because of a large reader response to this column, I regret that I did not clearly state that I do not support any government policy that allows illegal immigrants to enter our country.

Trick Or Treat Blues

October 2004

This column is being written the day after Halloween of 2003, and it is being written by a saddened writer. Halloween night came and went without a single call of "trick or treat" from a single child.

It all left me empty. To think we have lost such a fun night—not just for kids, but for some of us adults who found it a blast.

Not so many years ago, I greeted more than 100 delighted, squealing kids at my door. I went to great effort to join in the fun. Often, I rigged up a big speaker in the bushes by my front door. When I saw a kid approaching, I turned on a record that blasted out some terrifying screams and other scary noises of the night. My favorite kid was the one about age 6 who came dressed as a tough football player. He looked up at me and said: "You don't scare me mister. Trick or treat."

But Halloween went bad a number of years ago when some wacko in Detroit or Denver or somewhere gave a child an apple containing a razor blade. All that national publicity ruined Halloween forever. I blame three things: an imprudent press, paranoid cops and overreacting parents.

When my Halloween night visitors dropped to a trickle of kids, I sat at my desk in the *Lansing State Journal* newsroom and read a front page headline that said: "Lansing police investigate 19 reports of tainted candy."

I called the police chief and asked him to find out how many of those complaints were legitimate. A few hours later, he called to answer "none." The chief, Charles Reifsnyder, shared my lament, saying: "Yeah, Jim, I think you are right. We have parents scared to death at Halloween. We issue all kinds of news releases in advance and warn kids and parents. We even offer to set up inspection stations where we can examine and x-ray the candy. In all my 30-plus years on the force, I don't remember one proven case of such injury to a child."

The next year, I was preparing for the little ghosts and goblins when I heard a report on the radio from the East Lansing Police Department. As trick-or-treat night was underway, the radio warned East Lansing kids that someone was passing out apples containing broken glass.

Parents everywhere rushed their children back to the safety of their homes. Halloween was ruined.

The next day, I called the East Lansing police chief and asked how that investigation was going. Very sheepishly, he said: "We feel pretty bad about it all, Jim. I know how you feel about us cops ruining Halloween and I guess last night's episode proves your point. What happened was that a lady bought a bushel of apples to pass out to the kids. She put the bushel of apples on the floor of her garage. Her cat knocked over a fruit jar from a shelf. It broke and a piece of glass stuck in one of the apples. The poor lady is in tears. She is hardly a demon."

The sad part is a little episode like that can wreck a time-honored tradition. I asked the East Lansing police chief: "If I had not called to demand a follow-up to your glass-in-the-apple warning, would you have called the radio stations today to report that the previous night's warning was a false alarm?' There was silence on the other end of the line. Those who did not read my column that day went on believing that some demon passed out broken glass in apples to kids.

Parts of the Halloween period are horrendous, of course, as when Devil's Night produces so much fire and vandalism. When I was a teenage kid growing up in Strongs, Bill McLeod and I might have tipped over an outhouse, but we'd never have burned it. Our modern society is surely not as safe as it once was, but we have come to a very sad state when moms and dads are afraid to let their kids dress up as a ghost and yell "trick or treat" on a neighbor's front porch.

Birds Gone Bad

April 2005

What's good for the goose is often bad for mankind. What's good for the cormorant is downright devastating for Michigan's sport fishermen.

So, we have quite a phenomenon going on in our Upper Peninsula. Conservationists and environmentalists are calling for the execution of the above birds.

About 20 years ago, there was a national concern that the Canada goose was facing some kind of extinction. Today, the shoe is on the other foot and an exploding goose population has put a plague on beaches, golf courses and city parks.

In Sault Ste. Marie, the goose population along the St. Marys River grew to a disgusting state and everyone was up in arms. Several years ago, members of the Elks Lodge took drastic action to protect their beautiful digs along the river. Elks members decided to violate state and city laws to shoot geese and stack them up in the parking lot like cordwood. They invited conservation officers and city cops to come and arrest them. All lawmen left town. Who wanted to arrest 500 members of the Elks?

But that ploy and others created a new awareness of the problem and, for the past several years, there has been an annual goose-hunting season in downtown Sault Ste. Marie. During the 10-day season, designated shooters from the police and fire departments and local conservation clubs shoot geese. They kill hundreds of them each year—right downtown.

It all reminded me of a time several years ago when I heard the great Ernie Harwell broadcast a Detroit Tigers game which had been long-interrupted by rain. Ernie ran out of things to say and had to turn the broadcast back to the studio for music. As Ernie is an old friend of mine, I thought I'd help. I made up a story and mailed it to him. My story told of the king who took over the reign of his country and issued an order that there would be no hunting on his land. So the animal population grew and the deer were pooping in everyone's yard. The people rose up and threw the king out of office. Thus, for the first time in history, the reign was called on account of the game.

Ernie read my story on the air a few days later, and I heard about it from friends for weeks afterward.

Cormorants are the latest embarrassment for the conservationists. These huge birds, imported from China, have devastated Michigan lakes and streams where they each eat many pounds of fish per day. Large flocks of cormorants land on a lake and soon empty it of perch, bluegills and more. Because the birds are protected by law, they have no predators. They grow fat and many.

Now, for the first time, the feds, the state, and a Soo Indian tribe have combined in a project to destroy cormorants, which are eating up all the perch in the Cedarville and Detour area. They plan to shoot some and spread some kind of oil on the eggs at uninhabited islands where the birds nest.

Sportsmen, meanwhile, have not hesitated to shoot cormorants as conservation officers turn their heads.

A friend of mine, Al Jones, has a better idea. Al is a retired U.S. Corps of Engineers worker at the Soo Locks. "When the seagull population got so far out of hand at the locks, we noted they all nested on an uninhabited island in the waterway. So I put a pig on the island. The pig ate all the eggs and our seagull droppings were considerably reduced," he said.

Here in Michigan, we delight in seeing a rare bald eagle soar overhead. In Alaska, they hate 'em. They have thousands of eagles per acre in some areas where the eagles land on trash dumps. They also swoop down and grab cats and small dogs. When nobody is looking, Alaskan hunters shoot our national bird.

I don't know where I stand in all of this, but I can describe a little experience my wife, Darl, and I had last spring while camped in a remote fishing spot in Luce County. As most people know, geese mate for life. At our annual pike fishing trip there, we often see mom and dad geese with big flocks of babies. This year, we noticed a pair on our shore with no babies. Obviously, a fox, raccoon or pine marten got into their nest. Then we saw a pair arriving with only one little fluffy feathered baby about 6 inches high. Darl threw out some bread crumbs. All the adults stood back and nudged the little guy in to eat. They waited until the baby had its fill and then they ate. Could I have shot that little guy? Not likely.

Your Death Is Not News

September 2005

Why are daily newspapers suffering from a decline in circulation?

That question was recently put to me by a young journalism student. And while I am not smart enough to provide a profound answer, some things do occur to me as a longtime daily columnist and newspaper customer. All answers to that student's question are complex. It goes to competition from TV, Internet, magazines and radio. Mostly; it comes down to a competition for the reader's time.

In my early days at the *Lansing State Journal*, I was one of several rewrite people in the newsroom who wrote an obituary for every person in our circulation area who died each day. We took collect calls from the funeral directors and wrote an obit for every death—prominent or unknown persons.

Meanwhile, large papers everywhere were giving up that practice and charging classified advertising rates for obits. Death was not news, and a family had to pay hundreds of dollars to get mom's obit in the paper—unless she was famous.

I recall the day the *Lansing State Journal* adopted that policy and bragged that it was the last big paper in Michigan to stop printing obits free. That was a sad day for many of us old-timers in the newsroom.

I am still troubled by that decision. I could see a charge for printing a wedding announcement, but my goodness, isn't death news anymore? Must you be a celebrity to get an obituary?

All that hit home hard for me one day last March when a friend died of a heart attack in his sleep at a travel trailer park in Port Isabel, Texas. The friend, Ray Drake, retired about 15 years ago as an air traffic controller at Lansing's Capital City Airport. As supervisor of air traffic controllers there, he felt that most accidents occurred in landings, takeoffs and taxiing on the runway. So, he regularly made his men go down and ride with the snowplow drivers, ambulance drivers, and lawn mowers so the controllers could better understand the problems of the men working on the field. Ray's idea was so good that it was picked up by the Feds and made a rule for all airports.

On the day of his retirement, they closed the airport for an hour and had every airport employee and their equipment line up on the cement in front of the air traffic control terminal and salute Ray precisely at 1 p.m.

That wonderful, meaningful event did not make the newspaper 15 years ago. Neither did his obituary last March. Ray's wife Janice decided on a cremation in Texas and a memorial service in Michigan sometime later. I reported it all to the newspaper but it didn't make news, and, because no area funeral home was involved, it didn't even make the classified ads obit section.

Unless you are extra famous, you'll never have your death reported in your local daily paper. If I owned a big newspaper and asked a customer to pay a goodly sum for an annual subscription, I'd promise them a free obituary when they had a death in the family. Even if that didn't create a bigger circulation, it would surely return to what used to be a solid commitment to news.